D1158283

Eyewitness Accounts of the American Revolution

Diary of
Colonel Israel Angell

The New York Times & Arno Press

Reprinted from a copy in
The State Historical Society of Wisconsin Library

*

Reprint Edition 1971 by Arno Press Inc.

*

LC# 70-140852
ISBN O-405-01189-X

*

Eyewitness Accounts of the American Revolution, Series III
ISBN for complete set: 0-405-01187-3

*

Manufactured in the United States of America

77392

DIARY OF

COLONEL ISRAEL ANGELL

Diary of Colonel ISRAEL ANGELL Commanding the Second Rhode Island Continental Regiment during the American Revolution

1778-1781

Transcribed from the Original Manuscript

Together with a Biographical Sketch of the Author and Illustrative Notes by

EDWARD FIELD, A.B.

Historian of the R.I. Society of the Sons of the American Revolution

ILLUSTRATED

PROVIDENCE, R.I.

PRESTON AND ROUNDS COMPANY

1899

Copyright, 1899
BY
EDWARD FIELD

THIS VOLUME IS DEDICATED

TO

THE MEMORY OF MY GREAT—GRANDFATHER

Darius Thurber

A FIFER AND PRIVATE IN CAPTAIN WILLIAM TEW'S
COMPANY

OF

COLONEL ISRAEL ANGELL S REGIMENT

AND TO HIS COMRADES
IN ARMS

PREFACE.

THE diaries here printed are in six separate parts, five of them being the property of Malcolm H. Angell, Esq., of Etna, Bergen County, New Jersey, while the other (Part Two) is the property of a descendant of Colonel Angell in Rhode Island. The pages on which the entries are written are about three and one half inches wide by six and three quarters inches long. The sections or parts of the diary vary as to the number of pages, and are stitched together without covers.

Their general appearance is indicated by the fac-simile page accompanying this work. The whole diary has been carefully transcribed and copious notes added. It is hoped that these annotations will add to the interest of the diary itself, and be found useful in identifying and describing persons and places briefly referred to by the diarist.

In preparing the great number of notes which is contained in the work, I have been aided by many persons, but to name all would be beyond the possibilities of this preface; to all such persons, however, I return grateful thanks. I desire to particularly acknowledge my obligation to Malcolm H. Angell, Esq., for permitting me to have in my custody the parts of the diary owned by him, and to Mr. Harris W. Brown for the use of the other section under his control. To His Excellency Elisha Dyer, Governor, and to the Hon. Charles P. Bennett, Secretary of State, I am indebted for courtesies extended in securing for the work the illustration of the standard carried during the war by Colonel Angell's regiment.

In addition to the diaries here printed Colonel Angell has left two others: one of them describes the happenings on a journey to the Ohio Valley in 1788, the other a trip to Philadelphia in 1792 ; both these are of peculiar interest from the notes which the writer made on the condition of these localities at that early period.

EDWARD FIELD.

PROVIDENCE, R.I., October 4, 1899.

COLONEL ISRAEL ANGELL.

ISRAEL ANGELL was a descendant in the fifth gen-
eration of Thomas Angell, who came to Providence
with Roger Williams ; he was the son of Oliver and
Naomi (Smith) Angell, and was born in that part of the
town of Providence now included in North Providence,
Aug. 24, 1740.

He received more than the usual education afforded the
youth of that period, for his mother had been a teacher in
one of the country schools and was thus able to give her son
many advantages of learning. He seems to have been con-
versant with scientific subjects, was particularly fond of natu-
ral history, and in his later years made many notes on this
branch of science as he travelled through sections of the
country on public business. He is also said to have been an
enthusiastic student of astronomy.

At the very beginning of the troubles with the mother
country Israel Angell took an active part. When the army
of observation was ordered raised by the General Assembly
of Rhode Island in 1775, he was commissioned Major of the
regiment commanded by Col. Daniel Hitchcock. The regiment to which he was attached formed a part of the Ameri-

can army laying siege to Boston and bore its part in the events which subsequently transpired.

There is a letter yet preserved among the manuscripts of the Rhode Island Historical Society written by Israel Angell to his brother, dated at Prospect Hill, Dec. 1, 1775. It gives a clear idea of the character of the man who was destined to bear so conspicuous a part in the struggle for independence, and for that reason it is here printed :

PROSPECT HILL, December the 1st 1775.

Dear brother —

I take this oppertunity to inform you that I Still Enjoy that Blessing which is my health. God be Praised. and I hope that you and all yours Receves the Same blessing. I was inform^d. by Our brother Elish that there was no nails to be had in Providence but that you thought likely there was Some in Newport. and If there is Pray Brother. Send and git them and See that one Room is furnished this winter otherwise I Shall be very Discontented about my familey. and only Send to me and let Me know what Sum of money you Shall want to Carry on the Business and I will Send it as Soon as Possible. there is no Nails to be had in this Part of the world and what news We have I Suppose you will hear of long before this reaches You the Privatears from Marblehead have taken a brigg from England to Boston Loded with war like Stores ; one Brass 13 inch Morter Bead and all Compleat 2 Brass Six Pounders 2000 Kings Arms — a great Quantity of Cannon Shoot And cartridges for both Cannon and Small arms a Number of Carbines and in Short Every war like article that Can be Mentioned all which is a Comming out to Cambrig and other Places from the Sea Shore. there was a malenculy Affair happened a few days Past at — deadham

Col¹ huntingdon Wife from Conneticut hanged her Self there She was Governer Trumbels Daughter of Conneticut & Sister to our Commisarry general in Cambrig Brother I am much allarm^d At the News of the Conduct of the People in Providence And the towns adjecent to hear that they are likely to Rise in mobs on the account of Salts rising and Some other Small Articals I begg of Every honest and well ment Person both in town and country to Exert them Selves to The utmost of their Power to Surpress aney riotous Proceeding Among your Selves Especily at this time for God Sake Let us unite all as one in America if we dont. but fall at varance among our Selves, of all Gods Creation we Shall be the most Miserablest   So no more at Present

Your &c

To Hope Angell   Israel Angell
Esqr of North
Providence   Brother I am afraid you Can Never
                          Read the above lines as They was
                          wrote in a few minutes And with a
                          bad Pen and poor Ink.

Upon the formation of the Second Rhode Island Regiment Daniel Hitchcock was elected Colonel and Israel Angell Lieutenant-Colonel, and the regiment was despatched to join the grand army under Washington.

Upon the death of Colonel Hitchcock the command of the regiment was given to Angell, his commission being dated Jan. 13, 1777 ; this position he held until the First and Second Regiments were consolidated.

In August, 1777, his regiment was at Peekskill, N.Y., from which place he wrote the following pathetic letter to the Governor of Rhode Island:

Camp No 2 August 27–1777

Gentlemen, Pure necessity urges me to trouble you this once more in behalf of ye Troops under my command ; you will easily recollect that I have repeated my Solicitations before you on ye Subject of their cloathing as far as was decent.

I did, indeed expect when I came from Home to find my men poorly Habitted nor was I disappointed their Dress even exceeded for badness what I had imagined to myself.

Not one half of them can not be termed fit for duty on any immergency; Of those, who of them went with me on a late expedition near to Kings bridge many were bare foot, in consequence of which its probable they won't be fit for duty again for many week 5 of them there deserted to ye enemy which I have reason to beleive was principally owing to ye non fulfillment of engagements on ye part of ye State and what may be expected better than this that more will follow their example while they daily experience that publick faith is not to be depended on. In fine ye Regiment is scandallous in its appearance in ye view of every one — and has because of this incurred from surrounding regiments from ye inhabitants of Towns thro which they have lately passed, ye disagreeable and provoking Epithets of the Ragged Lousey Naked Regiment. — Such treatment, gentlemen, is discouraging dispiriting in its tendency : it does effectually unman ye Man and render them almost useless in ye Army I am sorry to have occasion to continue my complaint in their behalf but as I look upon it, a matter, not of Empertinence but of Inportance I cannot refrain in justice to them.

I pray gentlemen you would as speedily as possible inform me of ye result of your Deliberation on the Matter and let

me Know whether they are likely very soon to have relief.
If this is not ye case I shall look upon myself in Honour
Bound to make my Application some where else

I am gentlemen with all due Respect Your Honours humble Servant

Israel Angell Colo.

To his Honour ye Gov. & Council State R. I.

Colonel Angell participated in the battles of the Brandywine and Red Bank and was with the army during the
terrible winter of 1777–1778 at Valley Forge.

His regiment bore a conspicuous part in the battle of Monmouth, and soon after this engagement he with his regiment
was detached from the main army and sent to Rhode Island
to unite with General Sullivan in the operations against the
enemy at Newport, R.I.   For distinguished services at the
battle of Springfield, June 23, 1780, he was the subject of
special mention by General Washington in a letter to Governor Greene of Rhode Island.

Upon the consolidation of the two Rhode Island regiments Colonel Angell retired from the position he had held
so long.

By the Act of Congress of Oct. 3, 1780, this was
not to take effect until the first of January following, but it
seems that it was some months later than this before he
wrote in his diary that his days as a military commander
ceased.

Upon retiring from military life Colonel Angell returned
to his home in the town of Johnston, where he carried on his

farm and followed his trade as a cooper; at the same time he was granted a license to keep a public house.

His tavern was a popular place of resort and was widely known for its excellence and hospitality.

Late in life he moved into the town of Smithfield, where he died May 31, 1832, in his ninety-second year. He is described by one who remembered him as of "medium height, light complexion, auburn hair surmounted by a wig, blue eyes, a strong Roman nose, and straight as a ramrod." [1]

Colonel Angell was three times married and is said to have contemplated a fourth venture when death terminated his life. [2] In love and in war Colonel Angell was a conspicuous figure.

---

[1] Statement in a sketch of the life and services of Col. Israel Angell read before the Rhode Island Society of the Sons of the American Revolution, Feb. 22, 1897, by Robert P. Brown, Esq.

[2] His first wife was Martha Angell, his second cousin, who died March 16, 1793. By her he had eleven children:

		Born.
Mary	. . . . .	June 17, 1766.
Elizabeth	. . . .	April 27, 1768.
Sarah	. . . . .	October 17, 1769.
Asa	. . . . .	August 24, 1771.
Abner	. . . . .	February 21, 1773.
Israel	. . . . .	September 12, 1775.
Martha	. . . . .	August 23, 1779.
Naomi	. . . . .	September 1, 1781.
Ruth	. . . . .	May 10, 1785.
Stephen	. . . . .	July 4, 1787.
Oliver	. . . . .	December 1, 1790.

His second wife was Susannah Wright and by her he had six children:

" He had seventeen children, eleven by his first wife and six by the second, and of the seventeen, thirteen reached maturity and eight became octogenarians.''

He was buried in the family graveyard on his old farm in Johnston on the South Scituate road. For years this ancient burying-place has been abandoned and neglected, and the mutilated marble stone which marked his last resting-place, when the writer visited the spot a year or so ago was lying broken upon the ground. An iron marker of the Sons of the American Revolution has been placed over the spot by the Colonel's great-grandson, Harris W. Brown, Esq.

His military record as compiled by Heitman in his " Officers of the Continental Army " is as follows :

" Angell, Israel (R.I.), Major of Hitchcock's Rhode Island Regiment, 3d May to December, 1775. Major 11th Continental Infantry, 1st January to 31st December, 1776. Lieutenant-Colonel 2d Rhode Island, 1st January, 1777. Colonel, 13th January, 1777; retired 1st January, 1781. (Died, — May, 1832.)''

Such in brief is the history of the man whose diaries are here presented. His conspicuous service, his gallantry and

		Born.
Luther	May 11, 1794.
Infant son	February, 1794, died young.
Susannah	January 23, 1798.
Mehitable	January 31, 1800.
Henry	May 21, 1802.
Isaac	January 20, 1809.

The third wife was Sarah Angell, the widow of Richard Angell. (Angell Genealogy, page 80.)

bravery, demand more recognition than is now or has here-tofore been given him. No adequate history of his life has ever been written, but fugitive sketches have, from time to time, appeared in various publications in which his services have been briefly told. Some years ago a descendant [1] secured from various sources most of his private papers, the service sword which he had carried so honorably through the war, and many other relics and mementoes, for the purpose of using them in preparing a proper record for publication. They were all taken without the country, but ere they could be put to this purpose the person in whose custody they were died, and all this valuable material has been lost. No portrait exists to preserve the features and appearance of this striking personage in the history of the War for Independence.

---

[1] Hon. Anson Burlingame.

DIARY

OF

COLONEL ISRAEL ANGELL

OF THE

SECOND RHODE ISLAND REGIMENT OF THE
CONTINENTAL LINE.

The standard of which this is a photographic reproduction was borne by Angell's Second Rhode Island Regiment during the American Revolution until its dissolution. It is preserved with that of the First Rhode Island Regiment in the State House at Providence, R.I. When these two regiments were consolidated, January 1, 1781, both became the colors of the Rhode Island Regiment. On February 28, 1784, Jeremiah Olney, the last Colonel of the Regiment, in behalf of the officers deposited these standards with the State for preservation. The proceedings and correspondence relative to the matter may be found in the "Rhode Island Colonial Records," Vol. X., p. 14.

PART ONE.

THE diary of Colonel Angell begins with the twentieth of August, 1778. The regiment which he commanded was then encamped at Tiverton, R.I., and formed a part of the army under Gen. John Sullivan, then engaged in the operations against the British forces on Rhode Island.

It details the happenings from day to day during the siege, and terminates September 23, 1778, when Colonel Angell was at his home in Johnston on leave of absence by reason of sickness.

The regiment had then taken up quarters about a mile above Warren, where it was encamped.

August 20th, 1778. A cloudy foggy morning but broak away by nine o'clock and the Canon begun to play. Gov. Bradford [1] Come to my quarters this day and Dind with

---

[1] William Bradford, Deputy Governor of Rhode Island from November, 1775, to May, 1778.

us. I was ordered on duty to day and Marched of with a detachment of 500 men as a Covering party at five oclock P.M. and Releaved Colonel Wigglesworth,[1] the french fleet not being yet heard of[2] Spread great consternation in the Army.

21st. A pleasant Morning but Some foggy there was an Exceeding heavy fire from both Armys to day, with Cannon and Hoitzers we had but one man hurt and he had the Calf of his leg Shot away by a Cannon Shot as he was going to Carry his mesmates Some Vittles I was Releaved by Col. Jacobs[3] about 8 oclock in the evening.

August 22d, 1778. A Clowdy thick

---

[1] Edward Wigglesworth (Mass.), Captain Company of Massachusetts Matrosses, 29th June, 1776; Colonel Massachusetts Militia in 1776 ; Colonel 13th Massachusetts, 1st January, 1777 ; resigned 10th March, 1779. (Died 8th December, 1826.) — (Heitman's "Officers of the Continental Army.")

[2] Diary of Fleet S. Greene, written in Newport, in "Historical Magazine," 1860, Vol. IX., under date August 20, notes, "At 11 o'clock this morning a Fleet appeared standing off about W. N.W. with the wind at S.W: it is thought to be the French." The same period covered by this diary of Angell's is also covered by the Greene diary, and being an account of the happenings within the British lines is of peculiar interest in connection with Angell's statements. See "Historical Magazine," 1860, Vol. IV., 1–34, 69, 105, 134, 172.

[3] Heitman mentions a John Jacobs, Massachusetts, who was Lieutenant-Colonel of the 23d Continental Infantry. Colonel Jacobs is mentioned in the "After Orders" of August 15 as one of the Field Officers.

morning with a North East wind and Cold we had a great Number of Cannon Carried to the different Batteries last Evening in order to open upon the Enemy this morning, but the weather being thick prevented our beginning the fire so soon as we Should had the weather have been clear. on Circumstance I forgot to mention the night before last after I had finished my journal for that Day there was an Express come to headquarters from Count D^e Estaing the french Admiral who had arived and lay without the light hous [1] and yesterday we saw the Ships two of them had ben Dismasted in the late Storm one was the Admirals ship [2] she was totally dismasted the others had her Mizen mast Carried away, and her main top one Simmons from Providence was badly wounded by the Bursting of a Shell there was but litt firing to day to what there was yesterday.

August 23d, 1778. A thick morning and Cool, the Enemy flung Shells the Greatist part of the night past, and this morning the Batteries on our Side was opened on the Enemy and a most terrible Cannonade kept up during the day.

---

[1] Beaver Tail Light-house at southern end of the island of Conanicut (subsequently destroyed by the British).

[2] The "Languedoc."

I dind with Gen¹ Greene ¹ to day, the french
fleet Left us to day bound to Boston and I
think left us in a most Rascally manner and
what will be the Event God only knows we
had one man kill'd and one or two wounded,
one Eighteen pounder and one Brass ten inch
morter was split to day but kild no man.²
August 24th, 1778. A Smoking thick
morning the Enemy Continued throwing Shells
all the night past. and to day the Cannonade
Continued very Sevear I and Col Olney was
Curious Enough to measure all the Covered
way ³ which was 1512 yards. in the afternoon
we got our thirteen inch morter to play and
flung three Shell but did no execution they
broak in the air as the fues was two Short.
25th. A clear hott morning and a sevear
Cannonade and Bumbarding Still kept up and
Continued the whole Day, we got off some of
our heavier Baggage to day in order to make a
Retreat of the Island in Case necessity required

---

¹ Gen. Nathanael Greene, who had been detached from the main
army to coöperate in Sullivan's expedition.

² Rev. Manasseh Cutler, Chaplain of Titcomb's Regiment, says in
his diary under this date, " One man Killed by a cannon ball at one
of our guns; another died of the wound he received yesterday by
the bursting of a shell . . . Our people split one eighteen
pounder and one nine and a half inch mortar."

³ The covered way is shown on the battle map of Sullivan's
expedition accompanying this work.

it Major Blodget came to Camp to day from the westward but brought nothing new I sent off my marque and went and took quarters with Col. Livingston [1] and Major Huntingdon [2] at night we mustered all the teams we had and proceeded to the lower works in order to git off all the Cannon and morter as a Retreat was Determined upon.

August 26. Clear and Exceeding hott about Eleven o'clock there was a Allarm it being Reported that the Enemy was a Coming out but proved falls and we rested in peace this day.

---

[1] Livingston, Henry Beekman (N.Y.), Captain 4th New York, 28th June, 1775. By the act of 12th December, 1775, it was "Resolved, that this Congress will make a present of a sword of the value of $100 to Captain Henry B. Livingston, as a testimony of his services (at Chambly, S.C.) to this country, and that they will embrace the first opportunity of promoting him in the army." Major 3d New York, December, 1775, to rank from 2d August, 1775; Aide-de-Camp to General Schuyler, February to November, 1776; Colonel 4th New York, 21st November 1776; resigned 13th January, 1779. (Died 5th November, 1831.)

[2] Ebenezer Huntington (Conn.), served in the Lexington alarm, April, 1775; 1st Lieutenant 2d Connecticut, 8th September to 10th December, 1775; 1st Lieutenant 22d Connecticut Infantry, 1st January, 1776; Captain, May, 1776; Brigade-Major to General Heath, August, 1776; Major of Webb's Additional Continental Regiment, 1st January, 1777; Lieutenant-Colonel, 10th October, 1778; transferred to 3d Connecticut, 1st January, 1781; transferred to 1st Connecticut, 1st January, 1783; retained in Swift's Connecticut Regiment, June, 1783, and served to 3d November, 1783; Brigadier General United States Army, 19th July, 1798. Honorably discharged, 15th June, 1800. (Died 17th June, 1834.) (Heitman's "Officers of the Continental Army.")

27th August, 1778. Cloudy and rained a little this morning but Soon broke away and was hott we met with som misfortune last Evening. I had one Ensign and 14 men taken prisoners by the British troops as they was a Setting their sentries the Ensign was John Viol.[1] Genl. Varnum[2] formed an expedition against a picquet which lay near our right wing, which proved unfortunate being drove off with the Loss of one Lt and 3 privates I was the officer of the Day to day. three large Ships arrived in the harbor about

---

[1] Mrs. Williams, in her " Biography of Revolutionary Heroes," Providence, 1839, page 93, gives another version of Vial's capture, in which she relates, " He fought at the battle of Rhode Island in Sullivan's expedition, and was left on the island by mistake.

" Being on picket guard, they forgot to notify him at the retreat, and he fell into the hands of the British, and was kept for a time in one of the prison ships lying in the harbor of Newport."

These details are inconsequential, yet perhaps the diarist's account is more worthy of belief.

[2] James Mitchell Varnum (R.I.), Colonel Rhode Island Regiment, 3d May to December, 1775; Colonel 9th Continental Infantry, 1st January to 31st December, 1776; Colonel 1st Rhode Island, 1st January, 1777; Brigadier-General Continental Army, 27th February, 1777; resigned 5th March, 1779. Was also Major-General Rhode Island Militia. (Died 10th January, 1789.) (Heitman's " Officers of the Continental Army.") Also Colonel of the Kentish Guards, 1774. See Greene's " History of East Greenwich," pages 179 to 185; also same 169–176 for biographical sketch.

See also Cowell's " Spirit of '76 in Rhode Island," page 256. A poor portrait of Varnum in Stone's " French Allies," page 84. Updike's " Memoirs of the Rhode Island Bar. Boston, Thos. H. Webb & Co., 1842." Page 145.

two o'clock Suppos'd to be from New York
I din'd with Col. Greene [1] thro' day and spent
the Greatest part of the afternoon in Visiting
the Guard.

August 28th, 1778. A Clear Morning
and very Cool. Several Accidents happened
during the night past, in the first place we was
ordered to strike our tents and march of by
Eight o'clock in the Evening to the North
End of the Island. and the Order of March
given out. but the order was Countermanded

---

[1] Christopher Greene was the son of Judge Philip Greene and
Elizabeth Wickes Greene, and was cousin to Gen. Nathanael Greene.
He served as Major in Arnold's expedition against Quebec in 1775,
and was made a prisoner.

During the period of captivity he was, upon recommendation
of General Washington, appointed Lieutenant-Colonel of the First
Rhode Island Continental Regiment.

His military services, as compiled by Heitman, are as follows:
Greene, Christopher (R.I.), Major of Varnum's Rhode Island Regi-
ment, 3d May, 1775; Lieutenant-Colonel; taken prisoner at
Quebec, 31st December, 1775; Colonel 1st Rhode Island, 27th
February, 1777, to rank from 1st January, 1777.

By the Act of 4th November, 1777, it was " Resolved that Congress have a high sense of the merit of Colonel Greene and the
officers and men under his command, in their late gallant defence
of the fort at Red Bank, on the Deleware river, and that an elegant sword be provided by the Board of War and presented to
Colonel Greene."

He was killed 14th May, 1781, by Delancey's Tories in Westchester County, N.Y. For a particular account of the battle of Red
Bank and illustration of his magnanimity on this occasion see
" Christopher Greene, Hero of Red Bank," by Mary A. Greene in
the " American Monthly Magazine," Vol. II., No. 5, page 521.

and we were ordered to tarry on the Ground till further orders last evening I had one man kill'd by our own people a Sentrie on the right of one of the picquets discovering one of the Sentries on the left of the other picquet which formed the line of Sentries and chalinging him he either did not hear or refused to Answer and the other Sentrie fired on him Shott him through his knec and he Expired very Soon there was a Considerable of firing between the sentries.

August 29th, 1778. A Clear morning and Very Cool the (   ) Recd orders last evening to Strike their tents and march to the north end of the island. the advanced piquet was to come off at 12 oclock the enemy finding that we had left our ground pursued with all possible speed Come up with our piquet about sunrise and a smart firing begun, the piquet repulsed the Brittish troops 2 or 3 times but was finily obliged to retreat as the Enemy brought a number of field pieces against them the Enemy was soon check't by our Cannon in coming up to our main body and they formed on Quaker Hill and we took possession of Buttses Hill [1]

---

[1] Quaker Hill and Butts Hill are two hills in Portsmouth, R.I. They were both strategic points in the battle. For view of fort on Butts Hill see my "Revolutionary Defences in Rhode Island," opp. page 140.

the left wing of the brittish army was Compossed
of the hessians who Attackt our right wing and
a Sevear engagement Ensued in which the hessians was put to flight and beat of the ground
with a Considerable loss our loss was not very
great but I cannot assertain the number. I
was ordered with my Regt to a Redoubt
on a Small hill which the Enemy was a
trying for and it was with Difficulty that we got
there before the Enemy. I had 3 or 4 men
kill'd and wounded to day at night I was ordered with my Reg to lie on the lines I had not
Slept then in two nights more than two or
three hours the Reg^t had eat nothing during the
whole Day this was our sittuation to goe on
guard, but we marched off Chearfully and took
our post.

August 30th. A Cloudy morning and the
wind very high it rained a Considerable in the
night the Enemy Remained on their Ground
this morning two English friggats Came up
yesterday to prevent our retreat but could do
but little they Still Remained here. I was Re-
lieved this morning and got Some provisions
and being much worn out for the want of sleep
went to a hous and took a good knap there was
a Cannonade kept up to day and Some small
arms from the Sentries at night we Recd orders

to Retreat off the Island which we did without the loss of anything, this Retreat was in Consequence of an Express from Genl Washington informing Gen Sullivan [1] that the Brittish Ships of war and transports had sailed from New York Some days before.

August 31st, 1778. Our retreat off the Island was completed by three o'clock this morning it is Supos'd that the Enemy attempted a Retreat last Evening but after finding that we Had Retreated they Returned to their ground as it was late in the morning before they took possession of the forts we left one accident happened yesterday was forgot to be mentioned in that days journal Lt Arnold[2] of the artillery was killed accidentally as he had fired his Piece Stept off to see where the Shot Struck and Steping before the mussel of another Gun as the officer gave the word fire the ball went through his body blo'd him too peaces his Body hung togeather by only

---

[1] See "General Sullivan — a Vindication of his Character as a Soldier and a Patriot," by Thomas C. Amory, Esq., of Boston. "Hist. Magazine," 1866, Vol. X., Supplement No. VI.

"The Military Services and Public Life of Major General John Sullivan," by Thomas C. Amory, Boston, Mass., 1868.

"Biographical Sketch in General Sullivan's Indian Expedition, 1779," Camden, N.Y., 1887.

[2] Heitman's "Officers of the Continental Army" mentions Noyes Arnold (Mass.), 1st Lieutenant 3d Continental Artillery, 1st February, 1777. Died 23 August, 1778.

the Skin of his belly, one Arm was blown Clear off After we had Crost at howlands ferry we Encampt about a mile from Sd. ferry where we tarried this day at Night Rec'd orders to Strike our tents next morning and Embark on board our Boats and Land near Warren as Genl Varnums Brigade was to be stationed Between warren and Bristol. Genl Cornells [1] at Howlands ferry Genl Glovers [2] at Providence Col. Com^dt Green at warwick and Greenwich.

September 1st, 1778. We embarked on board our Boats this morning at Seven oclock Agreeable to Last Evenings Orders and landed about ten o'clock at Kickamuit bridg [3] near warren where we lay waiting for orders untill 4 oclock P.M. then marched to warren and pitched our tents and tarried that night this Day was Cloudy and Rained a little.

September 2d, 1778. A Cloudy Cold

---

[1] Ezekiel Cornell was a native of Scituate, R.I. In 1775 he was Lieutenant-Colonel of Hitchcock's Regiment in the Army of Observation. He subsequently was elected Brigadier-General, and was actively engaged in the military affairs of the State up to May, 1780, when his brigade was mustered out of service. He was subsequently elected to Congress and served with the same honor in civil affairs as had characterized his conduct in the military affairs of his native State.

[2] Gen. John Glover, of Massachusetts. He remained at Providence until July 7, 1779.

[3] Kickamuit River lies to the east of Warren and Bristol. Kickamuit Bridge crossed the river within Warren limits.

morning it rain'd very hard part of the Night past we Rec'd orders last Evening to march this morning at 7 oclock but our waggons not Cumming up prevented our marching untill the Afternoon then we Struck our tents and marched off to Bristol there Encampt on Bradfords hill.

Sept. 3d. A very Cold morning for the Season Col Olney [1] was much unwell with the ague in his face   I sent a Boat to providence to day for Cloathing and at night I took command of the piquet Nothing Extroardinary happen'd Except my writing this days journal in the manner I have jumping from one thing **September 4th, 1778.** An Exceeding Cold morning but Clear Col Olney set off for Providence soon after breakfast as he was Exceeding much unwell with ague in his face But nothing of consequence happen'd Dureing the day.

---

[1] Jeremiah Olney (R.I.), Captain of Hitchcock's Rhode Island Regiment, 3d May to December, 1775; Captain 11th Continental Infantry, 1st January to 31st December, 1776; Lieutenant-Colonel 2d Rhode Island, 13th January, 1777; transferred to 1st Rhode Island, 1st January, 1781; Lieutenant-Colonel Commandant, 14th May, 1781; served to close of war. (Died 10th November, 1812.) The 1st Rhode Island Regiment, after May, 1781, was also known as Olney's Rhode Island Battalion. (Heitman's "Officers of the Continental Army.") For biographical and historical sketch and silhouette see "Olney Genealogy," page 32; Stone's "French Allies," pages 448, 449.

Do 5th, 1778. A cool morning Q^r Master Carpenter Came into Camp last Evening with Some Cloathing for my Reg^t and this morning it was delt out to them. he allso brought 4 Chists of Arms for my Reg. which we delt out to the troops and Returned in our old ones there was a flag went from providence to Rhode Island to day and another from our Encampment went in by the way of Bristol ferry.[1] there was Several Cannon fired to day but what fired at is not known.

September 6th, 1778. Clear and hot this morning there was a firing of Cannon heard the night past and this morning there Came an Express from beadford[2] informing

---

[1] A ferry formerly connected the mainland to the south of Bristol and the island of Rhode Island. The island end is now called Bristol ferry.

[2] The attack on New Bedford was made on the evening of September 5, 1778, and before twelve o'clock the next day the British had destroyed " about seventy sail of vessels, many of them prizes taken by American privateers and several small craft; burned the magazine, wharves, stores, warehouses, vessels on the stocks, all the buildings at McPherson's wharf, the principal part of the houses at the head of the river, and the mills and houses at Fairhaven opposite."

This expedition against New Bedford was instigated by Sir Henry Clinton, and was carried out by General Grey, who landed with a sufficient force upon Clark's Neck at the mouth of the river.

After completing the depredations at New Bedford the marauders turned their attention to Martha's Vineyard, where they inflicted some damage and obtained large quantities of provisions for the army and fleet.

us that the brittish troops had landed and burnt beadford I dind with the Marquis de La ffiat and while we was at the table there Came another Express with four Deserters from beadford informing us that all the houses and Stores and Shipping were Destroyed at Beadford and that the troops were all Embarked on board of their Ships while I was at the Marquises my brother Jason [1] Came to me and brought the agreeable news that my family and friends were all well he set off for home in the Evening.

Sept. 7th, 1778. fine pleasant weather this morning I sent all my spare guns to the Store at providence in a boat by water allso sent a Serj[t] and a file of men to pawtuxet and Cranston after some Deserters who Deserted from me at the westward wrote Several letters which took up the forenoon I din'd with Gen Varnum and in the afternoon went on Duty taking the Command of the piquet at night we Recd orders to Move Boats enough round into warren river to move the Brigade over at once this order Come from Genl Sullivan and by the time we had got the men paraded the order was Countermanded.

---

[1] Jason Angell, born Oct. 7, 1748; married Caroline Jenckes, daughter of Dr. John; their children were Oliver, Jenckes, Naomi, and Jason.

Sept. 8th, 1778. Clear hot and Dry weather. A number of Cannon was heard to day and last night at a great distance to the Eastward but no intelligence where Col. Greene Came here to day from Greenwich but brought no news. neither was there any thing Extraordinary happend during the Day Lt Dexter of my Reg. was Tri'd to day for disobediance of orders.

Sept. 9th, 1778. A thick Cloudy Morning Q^r Master Carpenter went for providence this morning to procure some Cloathing for my Reg^t. it begun to rain about noon and was an Exceeding Rainy afternoon and Rained great part of the night but Cleared off before Day and was pleasant I din'd yesterday at Genl Varnums.

Sept. 10th, 1778. A Clear and pleasant morning the Boat returned from Providence early in the morning but got but few of the Articals sent for. I took the Command of the Picket this Evening 4 or 5 of my men who was taken prisoners on Rhodeisland Returned this evening and Brought word that they were all Exchanged and the remainder were at Providence and Ensign Viol was with them.

Sept. 11th. A Clear and pleasant Morning but nothing Remarkable happened the forenoon I sent Benjamin King[1] who had been a prisoner to my hous in Johnston and to major Fenners on business in the afternoon the brigade turned out and marched to Bristol town and manouvered on the Common by the Meeting hous one of my Regt and one of Col Sherburnes Reg was flog'd this Evening.

Sept. 12th, 1778. A Coald raw morning Cap Hughes Came[2] to Camp last Evening and

---

[1] Benjamin King, Corporal in Major Thayer's Company of Angell's Regiment.

[2] Thomas Hughes (as the name is invariably spelled in the Family Bible), only son of Joseph and Mary Hughes, was born May 3, 1752. The place of his birth is not now known, but family tradition states the family was of Scotch-Irish descent. In the Rhode Island Colonial Records (Vol. X., pp. 412 and 413) he is mentioned as of Freetown, Mass. There is some evidence to show that his father may have been Dr. Joseph Hughes (or Hewes), who removed from Attleborough, Mass., to Providence shortly before the Revolution. Thomas Hughes' name first appears upon the public records in October, 1776, as Second Lieutenant of Col. Israel Angell's Battalion (Rhode Island Colonial Records, Vol. VIII., p. 11), and he was among the officers recommended by General Washington to the Rhode Island General Assembly for the new establishment of the Continental Army, in the same month and year. (Rhode Island Colonial Records, Vol. VIII., p. 36.) He was chosen, in February, 1777, to be First Lieutenant, and at sometime between August and October, 1777, was raised to the rank of Captain. He served with Colonel Angell's Regiment throughout the war. In 1791 the Rhode Island General Assembly appointed Col. Jeremiah Olney and Capt. Thomas Hughes agents for the Proprietors of the Anaquacut Farm in Tiverton, which was set off to the officers and soldiers of the late Continental Battalion, commanded by Colonel Angell. These agents successfully petitioned the General Assembly to make up a considerable deficiency demanded of them by the purchasers to whom

lodged with me the night past. We all turned
out this morning at Revele Beating agreeable

---

they sold the land, and a resurvey was consequently ordered.
Rhode Island Colonial Records, Vol. X., pp. 412, 413, and 437.)

Captain Hughes married Feb. 27, 1782, Welthian (born Nov.
19, 1757, died 1844), eldest child of Col. Christopher and Anne
(Lippitt) Greene, of Centreville, Warwick, R.I.

The children of Thomas and Welthian Hughes were:

1. Mary, born Jan. 4, 1783; married Burrows Aborn and had
eight children, all of whom died unmarried.

2. Christopher Greene, born July 9, 1785; died at New Orleans,
La., July 22, 1815. (A sea captain.)

3. Phebe, born Sept. 1, 1787; married her mother's own cousin,
Jeremiah, son of (Judge) William and Welthian (Lippitt) Greene,
of Occupasnetuxet, Warwick, R.I. Her issue are the only living
descendants of Thomas Hughes.

4. Katy, born Aug. 16, 1789; died in infancy.

5. Sally, born Dec. 15, 1790; died unmarried.

6. Elizabeth, born Feb. 2, 1792; died in infancy.

7. John Luther, born Nov. 2, 1795; died Jan. 14, 1863.

John Luther Hughes was a prominent merchant and manufact-
urer in Rhode Island, and as a member of the Common Council of
the city of Providence was actively instrumental in devising, fram-
ing, and establishing the present public-school system of the city.
He was the first Secretary of the Rhode Island Mutual Fire Insur-
ance Company. His residence, at the corner of Washington and
Greene streets, has recently been demolished in order to place the
new Public Library upon its site, a fate most certain to have been
pleasing to one of his refined literary taste and public spirit. He
married Eliza Whiting, and had several children, all of whom died
young.

Thomas Hughes served throughout the War of 1812 with the
rank of Major. He died Dec. 10, 1821, at his home at Centreville,
R.I., in the northwestern part of the town of Warwick, and was
buried in the family burying-ground on the farm of his brother-in-
law, Col. Job Greene, near by.

In April, 1896, this burying-ground was abandoned and the bodies
removed to Greenwood Cemetery, Phenix, R.I., including the re-

to Gen Orders Mr Consider Luther^1 came to Camp this day a little past Noon and brought me word from my family that they was all well the Evening before and Saw old Mr Richard Waterman^2 at my hous Who informed him that their family was well   Mr Luther Din'd at my Marquee then went home nothing Extraordinary happened during the day.

Sept. 13th, 1778. A Cloudy Cold raw morning with the wind at Northeast but soon broake away and was a pleasant Day the Bri-

---

mains of Major Hughes, his wife, and maiden daughter, Sally. A marker of the Sons of the American Revolution has been placed at his grave, his being among the first fifty names drawn by lot by the Rhode Island Society of the Sons of the American Revolution for the purpose of marking the graves.

Thomas Hughes was a small, wiry man, with reddish hair and blue eyes, of great energy and considerable executive ability. No living descendant is left to bear the name of Hughes, three grandchildren and six great-grandchildren of his daughter Phebe being all that remain of the family.

(Contributed by Miss Mary A. Greene, one of the great-grandchildren of Phebe Hughes Greene.)

Hughes, Thomas (R.I.), 2d Lieutenant 11th Continental Infantry, 1st January to 31st December, 1776; 1st Lieutenant 2d Rhode Island, 1st January, 1777; Captain, 23d June, 1777; transferred to 1st Rhode Island, 1st January, 1781, and served to close of war. (Heitman's "Officers of the Continental Army.")

^1 Consider Luther was a near neighbor; he died in 1814.

^2 Probably Richard Waterman, Jr., a great-grandson of the first Waterman and son of Esquire Richard and Abigail (Angell) Waterman, of Providence. He was born June 1, 1701, and lived in Cranston; the date of his death is not known, but in 1763 he was serving his fifth term as a member of the Town Council of Cranston.

gade marched to bristol town to the Meating hous[1] to attend Divine Servis when M[r] Thompson[2] Chaplin to the Brigade preached a sermon to the same, in the afternoon there was a funeral near the Camp at the hous where

---

[1] Probably the Congregational Meeting-house, the Baptist Meeting-house having been destroyed by the British May 25, 1778. For more than thirty years this church was under the pastorate of the Rev. John Burt. At the time of the British attack on Bristol, Oct. 7, 1775, Parson Burt, with others of the inhabitants, fled from the town; on the following morning he was found "lying dead upon his face in the midst of a field of ripened corn."

[2] Rev. Charles Thompson, the valedictorian of the first graduating class of Rhode Island College (now Brown University), and of which class General Varnum was a member, was ordained to the pastoral charge of the Baptist Church at Warren, July 3, 1771. He was born at Amwell, N.J., April 14, 1748, and was thus at the time of taking the pastorate twenty-three years of age. His ministry was eminently successful and the church increased in membership until the breaking-out of the war, when its effect was sorely felt. He was appointed a Chaplain in the Continental Army, which position he held until the year 1778, when, being at his home on the occasion of the British attack on Warren, he was captured and taken a prisoner to Newport, where he was confined for about a month and then released, but for what reason he never knew. ("A Discourse delivered at the Dedication of the New Church Edifice of the Baptist Church and Society, Warren, by Rev. Josiah P. Tustin, p. 129.") Charles Thompson, A.M.; ordained Baptist clergyman, 1771; preacher, Warren, R.I., 1770–71; pastor, 1771–75; Chaplain Continental Army, 1775–78; preacher, Ashford, Conn., 1778–79; pastor, Swansea, Mass., 1779–1802; resident, Charlton, Mass., 1802–03; trustee Brown University, 1795–1803. Born Amwell, N.J., April 14, 1748; died Charlton, Mass., May 4, 1803. (Historical Catalogue, Brown University, 1764–1894, p. 27.) "Among the prisoners (taken at Warren) were the Rev. Mr. Thompson, of Warren; Major Martindale, Mr. Edward Church, and a number of young men belonging to this town." (Fleet S. Greene's Diary, in "Historical Magazine," Vol. IV., p. 70.)

Gen Varnum Quartered it was an Antient
Woman mother of Capt Bradford [1] who owned
the land we were Encampt on

Sept. 14th.   A clear morning and nothing Extraordinary happened during the Day at
night I was the officer of the picquet and had
a plesant time to Visit the Guards Col. Olney's boy Come into Camp to day the Col set
off but meeting Col Sherburne [2] & Maj Huntington turned back as I had sent a boat for
Cloathing.

Sept. 15th.   A Clear Cool and plesant
morning and Nothing Extraordinary happened
During the day.   I spent part of the Afternoon
on poposquash [3] in the Evening L[t] Col Olney
Come into Camp from Providence and brought

---

[1] Mrs. Priscilla Bradford died Sept. 12, 1778, at the age of
eighty-five years.

[2] Henry Sherburne was appointed Major of the first battalion
of infantry raised in October, 1776, agreeable to an Act of Congress.
Soon after he was recommended by General Washington to the General Assembly of Rhode Island for a commission as Major for the
new establishment.   In May, 1777, he was Colonel of one of the
sixteen battalions raised by order of Congress, Dec. 27, 1776.
These regiments or battalions were known by the name of their
respective colonels.

[3] This name, Poppasquash, like all Indian names, has been
spelled in many ways.   In various books and deeds we find Poppasquash, Pappasquash, Pappossesquaw, Pappasqua, and Poppy-
Squash.   The weight of authority seems to be in favor of the first
form.   Respecting its derivation, no satisfactory information can be
given.   (Note in Munro's " History of Bristol," p. 66.)

news that it was Supos'd that the Enemy was
a coming this way and that three Brigades of
our troops was on their way here.

Sept. 16th. A pleasant morning Q^r
Master Whittlesey [1] Returned from Providence
this morning with 30 Blankets for the Regt
and a quantity of Shoes and Stockins and
westcots which we Imeditly Delt out to the
troops there was one Chist of Arms Come
which supplied Each man in the Reg with a
good fire lock we Rec'd orders this day to
march from the Ground we were now Encamped upon and Encamp about one mile and
a half above warren [2] but it being late in the
day before the Ground Could be Laid out we
Rec^d after orders to remain in our present Encampment.

Sept. 17th. It begun to Storm last Evening and has bin an Exceeding Stormy Night
with the wind at Northeast and this morning
the Storm rather seemed to increase the wind
rising and raining Exceeding hard and Con-

---

[1] Nathan Whittlesey, Q.M.S. in Capt. William Tew's Company, 1779.

[2] One regiment was encamped upon the field immediately south
of the rocks, upon the summit of Windmill or Graves Hill, where
are still to be seen the levelled and graded places where their tents
were pitched. The following winter the troops stationed in Warren were quartered in stores upon the wharves and in private dwell-
ings. (Fessenden's " History of Warren," 1845, p 98.)

tinued Stormey all the Day Which prevented our marching to the Ground alotted for us by yesterdays orders I din'd with Gen. Varnum and Spent Great part of the afternoon with the General.

Sept. 18th. A clear morning but Soon Clowded over we Struck our tent about 7 or 8 o'clock in the morning and marched off it Soon thickened up and rained a little we marched through Warren about one mile to the ground we entended to Camp upon and it set in to raining very hard but we Soon had all our tents pitched this proved to be the Clearing up Shower for it soon cleared off and was fine weather during the afternoon.

Sept. 19th, 1778. A Clear morning and very pleasant I was much unwell this morning being taking last evening with Cold Agurey fits pain in my head   I kept in Camp this day.

Sept. 20th. A Clear pleasant warm morning   I was Some better this morning thin I was yesterday and after breakfast sent a billet to the Gen[l] to know if he would let me go home for a day or two which he granted and after Dining set off taking Doctor Cornelius [1] and my boy

---

[1] Elias Cornelius (R.I.), Surgeon's Mate 2d Rhode Island, 1st January, 1777; taken prisoner at Staten Island, 22d August, 1777; escaped from prison ship in March, 1778; rejoined his regiment and served to 1st January, 1781. (Died 13th June 1823.) (Heitman's "Officers of the Continental Army.")

with me and ariv'd at my own hous before Sunset and found my family all well.

21st Sept. A fine plesant morning Benjamin Luther [1] Came to my house very early this morning for the Doctor to come and see his child which was very sick the Doctor went and returned by a little after sunrise and got his breakfast then went on for Providence from thence to Camp where he had Engaged to be by ten o'clock in the forenoon my Riding hurt me I was not so well as I was yesterday Benjamin Luthers child was thought to be a dying about twelve o'clock the neighbours was Calld in. my wife and myselfe went over but the Child had fits and lived the day out, in the Evening I sent my hors and boy to Doctor Slacks [2] to git him to Come and see M[r] Luthers Child.

Sept. 22d. A warm morning and Some foggy about half past 4 oclock Mrs Usher [3] Come and called up me and my wife to go over to Benjamin Luthers for their child was a dying we went as soon as possible but the Child was

---

[1] He was a son of Consider Luther.

[2] Dr. Benjamin Slack came from Massachusetts about 1750, and was a physician of considerable note in the towns in northern Rhode Island. He commanded the Captain General's Cavaliers during the Revolution.

[3] Mrs. Freelove Usher, daughter of Consider Luther.

dead before we got there I went home and tarried there the forenoon after dinner went to
Landlord Fisks[1] from thence to Mr Luther
then home I saw Doctor Fisk[2] at the Land-
lords who informed me that Byrans fleet had
arrived part in Newport he himself was there.

Sept. 23d, 1788. A Cloudy morning and
Rained some in the forenoon but the Storm
begun to increase about noon I and my wife
went to burying at Benjamin Luthers and imeadetly after we got there it set in to raining very
hard and Stormed all the afternoon and after
Buring was over we returned home and Elder
Samuel Windsor Com to my hous and tarried
all Night he and Elder Hopkins both Spoke
at the funeral.

---

[1] Joseph Fisk, son of Joseph, kept a tavern for many years in
the town of Johnston, on the Plainfield Pike, near the Scituate
line.   During the war he was a Corporal in the Captain General's
Cavaliers, a military company made up of men mostly belonging to
the town of Johnston.   He died June 18, 1793.   An inventory of
the tavern furnishings is in Providence Probate Records (Johnston),
Vol. I., p. 268.

[2] Caleb Fisk was a prominent physician and landholder in Cranston, R.I.   He lived on the Voluntown road near Bald Hill, in
Scituate, in a house still standing.   He was the son of John and
Elizabeth Fisk, and was born Feb. 24, 1753.   He was President of
the Rhode Island Medical Society, and left that Society a bequest
of $2,000.

PART TWO.

THE time included in the second part of the diary is from December 12, 1778, to February 11, 1779, and details the happenings during the severe winter while the regiment was encamped at Warren, Rhode Island.

December 12th, 1778. A Clear Cold morning after breakfast I sett of for the Camp at Warren Stopt Some time in Providence. Arrived in Warren in the Evening and found all well N.B. Ingaged to take the paper one Q^r.[1]

Decem. 13th, 1778. A Cold Stormy morning and Continued Storming all the day but Nothing Remarkable happened During the Day.

14th. it wet a little this morning but Soon Cleared off and was Cold nothing Remarkable happened this Day.

15th. Clear and Very Cold there was one Circumstance I forgot to mention in yesterdays Journal That is Birans Fleet Sail'd that

---

[1] Probably "The Providence Gazette and Country Journal."

day from Rhode Island [1] Lt Col Olney &
Major Simeon Thayer [2] Sett off this afternoon
for Providence, attended a general Court Martial of the Line. The Gen[l] Gave orders yesterday for a number of men to be furloughed
to day which kept me employed part of the
day in writing furloughs thus Ended the day
16th Dec. 1778. A fine and pleasant Day A garrison Court Martial Set this
day for the trial of two villains for attempting to Commit a Rape upon a ould woman

---

[1] "On the sixth of January, 1779, Admiral Byron's fleet, which
had been so long expected, arrived at St. Lucie, just eight days after
the departure of Count d'Estaing; and had it not been detained in the
harbour of Newport at Rhode Island by contrary winds and stormy
weather for fourteen days after it was ready to sail, it is probable,
either that the retreat of the Count d'Estaing to Martinique would
have been cut off, or that a general engagement must have been
risked in order to effect it." (Stedman's "History of the American
War" (Brit.), Vol. II., p. 91.)

[2] Thayer, Simeon (R.I.), Captain-Lieutenant of Hitchcock's
Rhode Island Regiment, 3d May, 1775; taken prisoner at Quebec,
31st December, 1775; exchanged, 1st July, 1777; Major 2d Rhode
Island, to rank from 1st January, 1777; wounded (lost an eye) at
Monmouth, 28th June, 1778; retired 1st January, 1781. (Died
14th October, 1800.) (Heitman's "Officers of the Continental
Army.") For account of his services in expedition to Quebec,
where he was captured, also a roll of his company, see Rhode
Island Historical Society Collection, Vol. VI., pp. 1, 102, and
Appendices, where his death is stated October 21. See also Cow-
ell's "Spirit of '76 in Rhode Island," p. 283; Providence Town
Papers in possession of the city of Providence; Military Papers in
Rhode Island Historical Society; and Revolutionary Rolls in office
Secretary of State, Rhode Island.

near four score their names were Perce & Pillars my Sergt Maj^r Proctor [1] was to be trid allso for forging a pass in my name the Court mett and adjourned untill the next day So the day ended with Nothing remarkable.

17th Dec. A Clowdy morning and Soon begun to Storm and was an Exceeding Stormy Afternoon, the Court finished the trials of Richard Perce who was ordered to Receave 100 Strips John Pillar to Receive 37. John Exceen [2] 20 but he was forgiven there Come News to day That L^t. Chapin with Six Men took a Brigg From Rhode Island laden with Forrag and Some Small matter of Spirits, the Brigg was about one hundred and thirty or forty tuns burthen and 13 hands on board.[3]

Decr. 18th, 1778. A Clear and Pleasant morning and was a Remarkable warm day for the Season Nothing Remarkable happened

---

[1] William Proctor. See Cowell's " Spirit of '76 in Rhode Island," p. 191; also Revolutionary Rolls in office Secretary of State.

[2] John Exceen, private in Capt. William Tew's Company of Col. Israel Angell's Regiment.

[3] This was the exploit of Lieut. Seth Chapin, of Col. Henry Sherburne's Regiment, in capturing in Rhode Island waters a British brig bound to New York. The expedition, consisting of Lieutenant Chapin and six men, embarked in a whale-boat from Little Compton, and by a bold stroke, without the loss of a life, took in the east passage the vessel and all her crew, including a lady passenger, the wife of Sir Guy Johnston. The whole party was safely landed at Seaconnet.

at Roll Call those prisoners under Sentance of
punishment [1] recd it Agreeable to the Sentence
of the Court Except the last who I pardoned.

Decr. 19th. A fine pleasant [   ]
as ever was known at the Season of the year
and nothing materal happened I dind with
Genl Varnum's Lady [2] there was a Small Dispute happened between Lt Thomas Waterman [3] of my Reg^t and a L^t in Col Webbs [4]

---

[1] The general form of punishment in the army was with the lash,
although in some cases offenders were hung and others shot. In
chastising a culprit he was first stripped to the waist and then
securely tied to a tree or post, then the chastiser stepped forward
and with a whip, formed of several small knotted cords, applied the
prescribed number of lashes. " It was always the duty of the
drummers and fifers to inflict the chastisement," and the drum-major
was required to attend and see that the duty was faithfully performed. (Thatcher's " Military Journal," page 186.)

[2] Gen. James M. Varnum married Martha Childs, the eldest
daughter of Cromwell Childs, of Warren, R.I. She died at Bristol,
Oct. 10, 1837, at the age of eighty-eight years. They were married
by the Rev. James Manning, Feb. 8, 1770.

[3] Thomas Waterman (R.I.), Ensign 2d Rhode Island, 1st January, 1777; 2d Lieutenant, 11th February, 1777; Regimental Adjutant, 10th August, 1777; dismissed 1st May, 1780. (Heitman's
"Officers of the Continental Army.") A list of officers and privates
in Colonel Angell's Regiment who have died or been honorably
discharged contains the name Thomas Waterman, lieutenant.
(See Cowell's " Spirit of '76 in Rhode Island," p. 195.) He was a
son of Lieut. John Waterman, Quartermaster of General Varnum's
Brigade, who died at Valley Forge, 1778; his grave is the only
marked grave now remaining in that historic locality ; a commission
has been appointed by the General Assembly of Rhode Island, and
an appropriation made, to erect a monument at the spot.

[4] Samuel Blatchey Webb (Conn.), 1st Lieutenant 2d Connecticut, 1st May, 1775; wounded at Bunker Hill, 17th June, 1775; Major

Regt concerning Rank on which Lt waterman
was ordered to Consider himself under an arrist
by Capt Williams [1] of s^d Regt. but they concluded to leave the matter to me and Maj
Huntingdon.

20th Dec. A fine pleasant morning and

---

and Aide-de-Camp to General Putnam, 22d July, 1775; Lieutenant-
Colonel and Aide-de-Camp to General Washington, 21st June, 1776;
wounded at Trenton, 2d January, 1777; Colonel of one of the sixteen additional Continental regiments, 11th January, 1777; taken
prisoner on the expedition to Long Island, 10th December, 1777,
and was a prisoner of war on parole until exchanged, December,
1780; transferred to 3d Connecticut, 1st January, 1781; Brevet
Brigadier-General, 30th September, 1783, and served to 13th November, 1783. (Died 3d December, 1817.) (Heitman's " Officers of
the Continental Army.") If he was not in service during the time
covered by this journal the regiment still bore his name.

The sixteen additional Continental regiments were raised by
the resolve of Congress, Dec. 27, 1776, and were known by the
name of their respective colonels. Webb's Regiment, which was
at this time a part of Varnum's Brigade, had the following field
officers :

Col. Samuel B. Webb, 1st January, 1777, to 1st January, 1781;
Lieut.-Col. William S. Livingston, 1st January, 1777, to 10th October,
1778; Lieut.-Col. Ebenezer Huntington, 10th October, 1778, to 1st
January, 1781; Major Ebenezer Huntington, 1st January, 1777, to
10th October, 1778; Major John P. Wyllys, 10th October, 1778,
to 1st January, 1781. This regiment was transferred to the Continental line Jan. 1, 1781, and was known as the Third Connecticut
Regiment.

[1] Samuel W. Williams (Conn.), 2d Lieutenant 6th Connecticut,
1st May to 18th December, 1775; 1st Lieutenant of Webb's additional Continental Regiment, 1st January, 1777; Captain, 23d
March, 1778; transferred to 3d Connecticut, 1st January, 1781;
retired 1st January, 1783. (Heitman's " Officers of the Continental
Army.")

very warm but soon Clouded over and continued the greatest part of the day after breakfast I rode to Bristol with Gen Varnum after
looking round and Viewing a Ship of war which
had come up against the upper End of the
Island Supposd to have come to releave one
of the Enemys Ships that had Lain there some
time but she had not gone they lay both togeather I arrived at my own Quarters by one
oclock & Dined with Capt Stephen Olney[1]
nothing Remarkable happened further this day.

Decr. 21, 1778. A very fine day and
nothing Remarkable happened Gen Varnum
went for Providence in the morning we Got

---

[1] Stephen Olney (R.I.), Ensign of Hitchcock's Rhode Island
Regiment, 3d May to December, 1775; 1st Lieutenant 11th Continental Infantry, 1st January to 31st December, 1776; 1st Lieutenant
2d Rhode Island, 1st January, 1777; Captain, 11th February, 1777;
wounded, at Springfield, 23d June, 1780; retained in Consolidated
or 1st Rhode Island Regiment, 1st January, 1781; wounded at
Yorktown, 14th October, 1781; resigned 1st May, 1782. (Died
23d November, 1832.) (Heitman's " Officers of the Continental
Army.") Also Ensign in John Angell's Company, Army of Observation, 1775. See also " Lives of Barton and Olney," by Catherine
Williams; Cowell's " Spirit of '76 in Rhode Island," pp. 236, 237 ;
Stone's " French Allies," pp. 440–444, where is also a muster roll of
his company at Yorktown, p. 445, and a portrait, p. 440; biographical and genealogical sketch and portrait in Olney Genealogy, p.
42. His grave is in the old family graveyard on the farm where
he died in North Providence, and is marked by a handsome slate
stone on which is inscribed at length his service during the war.
An iron marker of the Sons of the American Revolution was
placed upon his grave in September, 1895, by the editor.

one guard hous finished to day At night it Clowded over and in the Evening begun to rain.

22d Dec., 1778. A Cold and uncomfortable Morning it cleared of in the night with Snow about over Shoe it Continued an Exceeding Cold day and Nothing remarkable happened Gen[1] Sullivan Sent an order [1] for all the Musicians to attend at Providence as the Band belong'd to Col. Webbs Regt. Major Huntington put himself in a most violent passion on the mater Swore the order was a dam'd rascally one if the Gen[1]. did give it.

23d Dec. it still Continues Extreme Cold

---

[1] General Order, 22 December, 1778. . . . "The Musicians of General Varnum's and Colonel Jackson's Bands to repair immediately to Head Quarters with their Instruments, Blankets and necessary Baggage for Tarrying one Week.

"The Commanding Officers of General Varnum's Brigade, and of Colonel Jackson's Detachment will send with them the best Drum and Fife from each Band. General Glover's Brigade to furnish two good Drums, and Fifes.

"The Barrack Master immeaditly to furnish a good convenient Room for those Musicianers.

"Major Flagg will attend them at such Times as he may think proper; and instruct them in Musick.

"The Commissary will supply them with Provisions, and One Jill of West India Rum per Day and more when he may find it Necessary.

"The Quarter Master will immediately furnish the necessary cooking Utentils for the Bands.

"The Adjutant General to forward Copies of these Orders to Warren, and Pawtuxet immeadiately."

I Sent a boat to Updikes new town [1] today for to get 200 pair of Shoes.

24th Decr., 1778. This morning was Extreme Cold the river in Warren was all froze over I sent to the barracks as soon as it was light to inform them that they need not turn out, as I was sure that they must freeze I had orders from the Genl to send a boat to Providence but the river being froze over was obliged to send a waggon won fortunate circumstance happen'd a Gentleman from beadford Come to Camp and brought 288 pair of shoes Which I bought for my Reg^t at 25 shillings p^r Pair, which Amounted to 1200 Dollars So ended the Day as Sevear as it begun on circumstance I forgot to mention that is Two of Col^o Livingstons men froze to death two nights past on Prudence Island they got lost a coming from Providence in a boat bound to Bristol in a Snow Storm there was Six in the Boat two perished the others survived.

December 25th, 1778. An extreme Cold Day I dind with Parson Thompson the day Ended with nothing Remarkable Capt Tew [2] and lady arrived in Garrison.

---

[1] The present village of Wickford, in North Kingstown.

[2] William Tew (R.I), Captain 11th Continental Infantry, 1st January to 31st December, 1776; Captain 2d Rhode Island, 1st January, 1777; retired 1st January, 1781. (Heitman's " Officers of

26th Dec., 1778. A most tremendous Stormy morning with dry Snow and a Violent high wind from the N. E. which continued the whole day and if I Ever saw one Storm worse than another this was the worst it being Extream Cold, never known Colder.[1]

27th Decr. Sevear and Cold but the Storm had Ceast in the night and it cleared away to day the Soldiers barracks many of them were almost blown full of snow the Day Ended with nothing Remarkable Except [   ] was Drifted so there was no stiring.

28th Dec., 1778. A fine clear morning

---

the Continental Army.") Captain Tew was a son of James and Anne (Arnold) Tew, of Newport, R.I., and was born April 5, 1745. He married Sarah, daughter of Jonathan Wilson, and died Oct. 31, 1808. At the time of his death he was a member of the Legislature of Rhode Island, President of the Newport Town Council, and a member of the " Society of the Cincinnati." He followed the business of a clothier in Newport.

[1] This was the storm known then and since as the " Hessian snow-storm," during which a great many German and British soldiers were frozen to death; the date of its occurrence is given as December 12 and 22, but from this journal it appears that this extreme weather continued until the 28th.

" Dec. 28 (1778), upwards of fifty people are said to have perished, chiefly soldiers, in a very heavy snow-storm which begun on the 25th, in the evening, and continued to morning; among which, one Hessian captain, two of the Anspach soldiers, and others." (Diary of Fleet S. Greene, Newport, in " Historical Magazine," 1860, p. 136, Vol. IV.) Abial Weaver, a private in Captain William Tew's Company, was badly frozen while on sentry duty and was an invalid thereafter.

but very Cold Col Olney arrived in Camp
about ten o'clock after freezing his feet some
he left Providence yesterday about 9 oclock
and had likd to have perished in crossing the
ferry [1] Maj Thayer arrived a little after Sunset.

29th Dec. A Pleasant day and nothing
Remarkable happened.

30th Dec. Pleasant this day being a day
Set a part for thanks Giving [2] I and Major
Thayer went out into the Country to Capt
Ebenezer Pecks [3] in Rehoboth there Din'd
and returnd to Camp in the Evening.

31st Dec., 1778. A fine day and nothing
Remarkable happened I was president of a
Court martial.

---

[1] The lower ferry, or the ferry at Tockwotten, as it was more
generally known, was the most in use at this time; it was operated
by Caleb Fuller, and was sometimes called Fuller's Ferry. For
some time previous to 1777 it was closed to the public, for the
small-pox was raging in the town and one of the hospitals was
located near the ferry. But at this period it was in operation, and
had been for some time. (See Providence Town Papers, 1205, 1207,
1353, 15059).

[2] "In 1778 Congress appointed both a spring fast, April 22,
and an autumn Thanksgiving, December 30." This day (December 30) was observed, also, as a day of thanksgiving by the
authorities in the States of Massachusetts, New Hampshire, Rhode
Island, Connecticut, and Vermont. (See "Fast and Thanksgiving
Days of New England," pp. 344 and 504.)

[3] Ebenezer Peck, "a man of public influence and distinction,"
then living in the northeasterly part of Rehoboth, near Great
Meadow Hill, on a branch of the Palmer River. He had a son,
Ebenezer, who died in the army. (Peck Genealogy, p. 49.)

January 1st, 1778 [1779]. fine weather
still continues the Court martial met to day at
9 oclock agreeable to adjournment & Proceeded
to business this day we received the Melen-
cully news of a great number of Semen a per-
ishing in the late Storm on the Eastern shore
one privateer from this place was lost one man
and his team of five cattle all perished on Boston
Neck[1] and three French gentlemen who had
been out into Roxbury and returning to boston

2d January, 1779. A fine plesant day
the Court Martial finished their business and
adjourned without time.

3d January. A Clowdy day my Regt
was mustered to day at Eight oclock in the
morning Nothing Remarkable happened it
rained a little in the afternoon

4th January. A Clowdy raw day in my
journal of the first day of this month is mention'd the news of a mellencully affair happening to the Eastward in the late Storm Since
which we have got the Porticulars of what Suffered on board the General Stark[2] Priveteer

---

[1] This does not refer to Boston Neck in southern Rhode Island,
but at Boston, for under the date Dec. 28, 1778, General Heath, in
his Memoirs, writes: "A waggoner, his horse and four oxen were
found frozen to death near the dyke, on Boston Neck; they perished
in the severe cold storm on the preceding Saturday evening."

[2] In a statement of the shipping lost during the war, up to Jan. 1,
1783, belonging to the inhabitants of Warren, is mentioned "Sloop

and the priveteer Called Genl Arnold [1] the first mentioned vessel lost 19 men the last 73 who all froze to death I furnished my Regt to day with their new hatts all bound and they made a grand appearance on the Parade being as well cloathed as any troops in the Servis.

5th January, 1779. A Clowdy Cold morning after breakfast Lt Col Olney went of for Tiverton being warned there for Court Martial but nothing remarkable happened during the Day.

6th Jany. Tolerable good weather for winter Maj. Thayer went for Providence to day and about 8 o'clock in the evening Lt Col Olney Returned having finished the Business he went upon

7th Janry. This day the proceedings of the Court Martial [2] where I was president

---

General Stark (privateer) Pearce 120 tons." (See "History of Warren," Fessenden, Supplement, p. 101.) This vessel, in 1778, was the property of Nathan Miller and others (see Rhode Island Colonial Records, Vol. VIII., p. 434).

[1] The privateer "General Arnold" drove on shore near Plymouth, and bilged; eighty of the crew perished; the survivors were much frost bitten. (Heath's Memoirs, p. 200.)

[2] General Orders Providence 5th Janry, 1779. . . . "At a Brigade Court Martial held at Warren by order of Brigadier-General Varnum, of which Colonel Angell was President. Ensign Hamlin, of Colonel Samuel B. Webb's Regiment, Try'd for neglect of Duty, and absenting himself from the Garrison, without leave: Found Guilty, and sentenced to be discharged the service. The

was made known as the Gen¹ had approv'd

General approves the sentence and orders it to take place immeadiately.

" Ensign Frothingham, Try'd by the same Court, for absenting himself from the Garrison, without leave : Found Guilty, and sentenced to be discharged the Army. The General approves the sentence : but upon the recommendation of the Court, restores him to his former Rank.

" Lieutenant Price of Colonel Elliotts Regiment Try'd by the same Court, for absenting himself from the Garrison three Days without leave, and for associateing with the Waggon Master, and Forage Master of the Brigade : Found Guilty, and sentenced to be discharged the service. The General approves the sentence, and orders it to take place immeadiately.

" Captain Loiseaux, and Lieutenant West of Colonel Livingstone's Regiment, Try'd by the same Court for behaving unbecoming the carracter of Gentlemen in fighting before the Soldiers, and for being Drunk : Captain Loiseaux found Guilty by the Court, and sentenced to be discharged the service. The General approves the sentence, and orders it to take place immeadiately. Lieutenant West is found not Guilty. The General orders him releas'd from his arrest.

" Captain David Dexter of Colonel Angell's Regiment Try'd by the same Court, for leaving 'his Post on the 25th of December 1778, and not returning 'till the 29th for behaving unbecoming the Carracter of an Officer, and a Gentleman, in frequently associateing, with the Waggon Master of the Brigade : Found guilty by the Court, and sentenced to be discharged the service.

" The General approves the sentence, and orders it to take place immeadiately.

" The Court Martial in consideration of Captain Dexter's long Services, and sufferings in the American cause, and the sense they have, of his bravery, and activity, have recommended him, to be entitled, to the same priviledges, as those who are left out in the new arrangement of the Army. The commander in chief is sensibly mortified that he cannot by complying with the recommendation of the Court, evince the regard he has for that Officer's former Services, Activity, and Bravery. The sentence being for a dismission, and the recommendation, not for a restitution to his command,

the Same Capt David Dexter [1] was Discharg'd
the Service, Capt Lorsoiux [2] of Col James
Livingstons Regt was allso Dischd Lt Whillys
of the same Regt Acquitted Ensigns Hamlin [3]

---

he cannot possibly be intitled to any future Advantages; and the
declareation of it in orders would be deem'd a nullity, and could
have no good effect in his favour.

" All the Field Officers in Town are desired to be at Head Quarters this evening at Six o'Clock."

[1] David Dexter (R.I.), Ensign of Hitchcock's Rhode Island
Regiment, 3d May to December, 1775; Captain of Babcock's
Rhode Island Militia Regiment, 15th January, 1776; appointed
Brigade-Major, 9th October, 1776; Captain 2d Rhode Island, 11th
February, 1777; deranged 1st April, 1779. (Heitman's "Officers
of the Continental Army.")

[2] From General Orders, 5th December, 1778. "At a General
Court Martial of which Colonel Angell was President: was tryed,
Captain Augustus Loizcan, for Cutting a Tent, of Public Property,
and making Knapsacks of it; for exchanging bad Firelocks for
good ones out of Public Stores, and selling them, for stealing
Soldiers Provision, speaking defamatory of the Officers, of Colonel
Livingstone's Regiment; and for threating Lieutenant Nichols's
Life; found Guilty, in part, and Sentenced to be dismis'd the
Service : But, in consideration of his former sufferings, and Services
in the American Cause, his Bravery, and former good Conduct,
and upon the recommendation of the Court Martial, the Commander in Cheif, Orders him to be releas'd from his Arrest, and
Orders him to return to his Duty."

Loisau, Augustine (N.Y.), Captain 1st Canadian (Livingston's)
Regiment, 18th December, 1776, to rank from 20th November,
1775; dismissed 5th January, 1779; name also spelled Loizeau and
Loiseau. (Heitman's "Officers of the Continental Army.")

[3] Daniel Hamlin (Conn.), Sergeant of Webb's additional Continental Regiment, 24th May, 1777; Ensign, 16th May, 1778; dismissed January, 1779. (Heitman's "Officers of the Continental
Army.")

and Frothingham [1] both of Col S B Webs Regt Discharged the Servis but froathingham was Restored Lt Price [2] of Col Elliots Reg^t of artillery Discharged in the Afternoon I set off for my own hous where I arrived just in the Evening

8th January, 1779. Spent the Greatest part of the Day at home went and spent a few hours with Major Richard Fenner [3] Returned and in the Evening Ointed for the Itch which I had bin so unfortinate as to catch but where was unknown to me thus Ended the Day with the Devil of a Stink

9th Janry. Clowdy raw and Cold to day and Soon begun to Storm and Snow'd Exceeding fast the greatist part of the afternoon at night

---

[1] Ebenezer Frothingham (Conn.), Sergeant of Webb's Additional Continental Regiment, 25th May, 1777; Ensign, 16th May, 1778; Lieutenant, 26th May, 1779; Regimental Quartermaster, 27th May, 1779, to June, 1783; transferred to 3d Connecticut, 1st January, 1781, and served to June, 1783; Lieutenant United States Infantry Regiment, 15th July, 1785; Lieutenant 1st Infantry, United States Army, 29th September, 1789; killed, 22d October, 1790, in action with Indians at the Miami Towns, near Old Chillicothe, Ohio. (Heitman's " Officers of the Continental Army.")

[2] Edward Price was 2d Lieutenant in Captain Sayer's Company, in Col. Robert Elliot's Regiment of Artillery. (Rhode Island Colonial Records, Vol. VIII., p. 355.)

[3] Richard Fenner, Jr., Major of the first regiment of militia in the county of Providence; commissioned Lieutenant-Colonel of same regiment May, 1779. (Rhode Island Colonial Records, Vol. VIII., p. 533-536.)

turned to rain I spent the day in the Neighbourhood.

10th Janry. A Rainy morning and Continued thawing weather all the day I was not
out of the Neighbourhood this day Nothing
Remarkable happened this Day.

11th Jany 1779. it Cleard off last night
and was very Cold this morning & Continued
growing Cold all the day I was to have
gone to Providence to day but a number of
people Comming in who had business with me
prevented my going So Spent the day at home.

12th Janry. A Clowdy Raw Cold morning but much warmer than it was the fore part
of the Evening past After I got my Breakfast
set of for Providence by the way of Wainscoot[1]
and tarried at my fathers the night following
Where I had the Pleasure of seeing all my
Brothers and Sisters[2] togeather Except my
sister Whipple[3]

13th Jany. A Tolirable pleasant morning
for winter after Breakfast I and my Brother
Jason Sett of for Providence where I spent the

---

[1] Wanskuck, near Providence.

[2] Colonel Angell had three brothers and two sisters: Hope Angell, Jason Angell, Elisha Angell, Ruth Angell, and Naomi Angell.
(Angell Genealogy, p. 80.)

[3] Naomi Angell married John Whipple. (Angell Genealogy, p.
39)

day. Capt Allen [1] of my Reg^t. was here and 35 men with him from my Reg^t there was a hundred from the Brigade a going on Some privat Expedition Suppos'd with Talbut [2] to Stick Another feather in his Capp I heard no news of Consequence this day, at night I Returned to my own hous by 9 o'clock P.M.

January 14th, 1779. An Exceeding Plesant day I Spent the day in the Neighborhood and nothing Remrkable Happened Isaac Angell [3] Come to See me today and I agreed with him to finish my hous

Janry. 15th. An Exceeding Cold and Clowdy morning with Snow as it had Snow'd part of the night I went in Serch of Some

---

[1] William Allen (R.I.), 1st Lieutenant 11th Continental Infantry, 1st January to 31st December, 1776; 1st Lieutenant 2d Rhode Island, 1st January, 1777; Captain, 13th January, 1777; transferred to 1st Rhode Island, 1st January, 1781; Brevet Major, 30th September, 1783; served to 3d November, 1783. (Heitman's "Officers of the Continental Army.")

[2] Col. Silas Talbot. In 1775 he was Captain in a company of the Army of Observation; October, 1777, promoted by Congress to the rank and pay of Major in the army, for "merit and services in a spirited attempt to set fire to one of the enemy's ships-of-war in the North River, last year." Nov. 14, 1778, recommended for a commission as Lieutenant-Colonel in the army for bravery and good conduct " in boarding and taking the armed schooner 'Pigot' of eight twelve-pounders and forty-five men in the east passage between the island of Rhode Island and the main." This exploit was performed Oct. 17, 1778.

[3] Isaac Angell was the son of Colonel Angell's brother Elisha, and was a house carpenter, and "is said to have been a very good workman." (Angell Genealogy, p. 85.)

Grain to day, but found none thus Ended the day with nothing Remarkable

January 16th, 1779. This Day was Colder than it had been for Severall days be¹ fore, I went to Providence and after finishing the business I went upon Returned to my own hous, it was reported in Providence that the party that was a going on the privat Expedition was a going to attack a Sixty Gun Ship of the Enemys

Jany. 17th. Clear and Very Cold I Spent the day at my own hous Capt Wm Arrow Smith ¹ who lived in my house Come from Boston to day and Brought News that one of our friggats had Returned to that port having taken Six prizes he also informs that mʳ Andrews Clothier General of Boston Shot himself dead a few days before by handling a pair of pistols

---

¹ The Providence town-meeting, March 21, 1777, remitted the tax of Edmund Arro Smith, amounting to 6s. 6d. In a bill of the town-sergeant, rendered to the town, there is the item under the date Dec. 26, 1785: "To taking charge of the things & Locking up the house of Mr. Edmund A. Smith, –0–1–6." Mr. Smith probably died about this time, for Jan. 6, 1786, a bill is ordered paid by the town of Providence for "Board of Mr. Edmund Arrow Smith's family, Mrs. Smith and four children, two weeks 3–0–0." Joseph Smith, a son, was bound apprentice to Ephraim Clemence; Thomas Smith to Daniel Davenport. Another son, Edmund Smith, died at sea on board the brigantine "Polly," Zephaniah Graves, master, in 1799. At the time of his death he was a minor, and an apprentice to Ephraim Clemence. In January, 1777, Edmund Arrow Smith was a private in the Independent Company of Light Infantry of the town of Providence. The similarity of names and the fact that no other reference is found to William suggests that the diarist might have been in error.

he had bought and one of them went of accidentaly and the Ball went through his head & he instantly Expired.

January 18th, 1779. Cold and Raw I was much unwell this morning and Spent the day at home   Isaac Angell Come to work for me to day.

Janry 19th. Extreem Cold but nothing Remarkable happened.

January 20th, 1779. Clear and Cold after Breakfast I and Capt Edmund Arrow Smith Set off for Providence by the way of John Waterman's Esqr and Daniel Thorntons I went to major Thayer's there fell in with Gen. Varnum Maj^r Thayer and Maj^r Box [1]

---

[1] Daniel Box was Brigade Major of General Varnum's Brigade; his left arm was rendered useless by a fall from his horse in December, 1776, when the army was quartered at Neshamany Ferry, Penn. In a list of invalids resident in Rhode Island, receiving a monthly pension for disabilities occasioned by the war, reported to the General Assembly of Rhode Island in February, 1786, it is stated the "wound so fractured the arm that several pieces of the bone have been extracted, and the wound is still open and the hand entirely useless." He died in 1801, leaving a widow, Mary Box, called also Polly, a daughter of James Field, son of John, 4th, of Providence, and great-great-grandson of the first John Field of Providence. The town of Providence frequently appropriated money for his support, stimulated, no doubt, by the following quaint appeals:

"To the Honourable the Town Council of Providence.
          "The humble Petition of Daniel Box Sheweth.
"Gentlemen
     "On the 22nd of Feby., 1786 I was admitted on the list of Continental Invalids, by a Committee appointed by the General Assem-

and Lt Carpenter, after Dining went on for
Warren where I ariv'd about seven o'Clock
in the Evening and found all well it Continued
Growing Cold all this day and by night was as

---

bly for that purpose, with an allowance of Ten Dollars per Month
and aproved of by the General Assembly then sitting in Providence.
As I have never yet received anything, there is due me on that
account 150 Dollars to the 22nd. of May, 1787. And having observed a late resolve of Assembly requesting the town Councils in
this State to supply their Invalids with specific articles, and pay-
ment to be made for the same out of the continental Taxes, but not
hearing of anything in this Town having taken place in consequence
of said resolve, I am induced to lay my distressed circumstances
before you, Praying you to take them into your serious consideration, and if possible to grant me some reliefe.

"I have been rendered uncapable for near two years past, to procure my self and family even the common necessaries of life, during
which period necessity has obliged me to dispose of all my little
moveables, my beding and wearing apparel not excepted, to procure necessaries for the support of nature; I have nothing more to
part with, and am absolutely suffering both in want of foode and
raiment, not having a single shirt to shift my self. To innumerate
all my sufferings is to cutting for a man of feeling, and what is related already I hope will be sufficient to induce the Honourable
Council to do something in my favour. I rely, Gentlemen, on
your goodness, beging God to keep poverty from the door, both of
you and yours, will ever be the fervent Prayer of your Humble
Petitioner

"Daniel Box

"Providence June 4th 1787"
Providence Town Papers, No. 4236.

"Providence Novm^r　　1787
"To the Honble the Town Council

"The Humble petition of Daniel Box. Sheweth
"Gentlemen

"It is with the greatest reluctance and sorrow, my necessitys
obliges me to crave your farther assistance, respecting my Contin-

Sevear as Ever known Capt Smith who Come to providence with me went for Boston and bound to [   ]

21st January, 1779. As Cold a morning as Ever was known and Remained so the Day but Nothing Remarkable happened.

22d. it Still remains Sevear Cold Some Difficulty arose in the Reg. Occationed by the Serg^t going out of their Quarters Contrary to

---

nental allowance as an Invalid. But when I consider your readiness to assist me on a former like occasion, I have not the least reason to doubt, but the same spirit of Benevolence, is still predominant. Especially when you consider the Inclemency of the approaching season. Heavens what a prospect! for a man every way unprovided for the onset. The approach of winter makes my necessitys the greater, as it requires many expensive articles in a family, necessary to its comfort, that is not so much wanted in the more clement season, likewise a number of small debts, which is reasonable to suppose, I must have contracted, during a two years indisposition, which I want very much to satisfy. Upon these considerations, and many others to numerous to mention, tho of equel weight; I in the most humble manner beseech the Honble Council, if it is not in their power to grant me an order for the whole ballance due, they will let it so far exceed the former grant, as the Summer exceeds the winter, or in that proportion.

" Upon your goodness Gentlemen rests all my hopes.

" In the meantime be pleased to except the unfeigned thanks of a heart full of gratitude and love for your past favour, and that the gates of plenty, honour, and happiness, may be ever open to you and yours, will ever be the constant prayer of your much obliged humble petitioner. &c.

" Note/ there will be due me the 23 of Novm^r 210 Dollars.

" Received by your last order on a Count   — 30   "

" Ballance   180 "

Providence Town Papers, No. 4615.

Orders. at night my self and Col. Olney Spent the Evening at Gen¹ Varnums Q^rs with Govenor Bradford and a Number of Gentlemen

I Recd a letter in the Evening informing me that there was a movement of the Enemy the letter was from Col Shearburne.

January 23d, 1779. Much warmer this morning then it had been before in Several days about 5 o'clock this morning there was a firing heard on the Western Shore, the flashes of the Guns was seen from this post, but what was the occasion or what has been Done is not yet known Gen¹ Varnum & Maj^r Thayer Come to the garrison this Evening from Providence but had heard no news of the above S^d firing thus Ended the day.

24th. A Clowdy wet morning and warm but Nothing Remarkable happened Col. Olney went to Providence to day.

January 25th, 1779. Clowdy weather and Raind hard in the afternoon.

26th. A Clear morning And warm but soon Clowded over Lt William Littlefield [1]

---

[1] William Littlefield (R.I.), Ensign 12th Continental Infantry, 1st January to 31st December, 1776; 1st Lieutenant 2d Rhode Island, 1st January, 1777; Captain-Lieutenant ——; discharged 20th June, 1780. (Heitman's " Officers of the Continental Army.")
The office of Captain-Lieutenant, so frequently found mentioned

January 23rd – 1779

Much warmer this morning then
it had ben before in Several days.
about 5 oClock this morning there
was a firing heard on the Western
Shore, the flashes of the Guns was
Seen from this post, but what
was the occation, or what has ben
Done is not yet known. Genl
Varnum & Majr Thayer Come to the garrison this
Evening from Providence. but had
heard no news of the above fir=
=ing. thus Ended the day ———

24th

A Cloudy weet morning and warm,
but Nothing Remarkable
happend. Coll Olney went to Prov=
idence to day

Returned this Evening from the Grand Army but brought no news of Consequence

27th. A Snowy Morning and had Snow'd Greater part of the Night past but was not very Cold it remained Clowdy all the day but ceast Storming about Noon nothing Remarkable happened this day Col. Olney Returned from Providence today.

28th January, 1779. A fine Clear and Plesant morning in the Afternoon Col. Webbs Regt. Mutinied [1] and turned out under Arms

---

in the rolls of the Revolutionary War, is here explained for the reason that its significance is not generally understood. Gen. Horatio Rogers, in his explanatory chapter to Hadden's " Journal and Orderly Books, 1776–1778," discusses the office and its rank in the British army, and as the American army was organized on practically the same plan, his statements apply equally well. " Each of the three field officers," he says, " was supposed to command a company, so that a regiment of ten companies would have but seven captains; but as the colonel rarely or never served with the regiment, there was an officer styled a captain-lieutenant who commanded the colonel's company. Prior to 1772 this was a distinctive grade between lieutenant and captain; but in that year an order was issued giving a captain-lieutenant the rank of captain; though the ' Captain-Lieutenant and Captain,' as he was afterwards designated in the Army Lists, was always the junior captain." Such was William Littlefield, of Angell's Regiment, in 1779; unlike the practice in the British army, Colonel Angell served almost continuously with his regiment.

[1] Mutinies among the Continental troops were not of infrequent occurrence. The troops were mostly incited to this disorder by the lack of pay and rations. May 29, 1780, two regiments of Connecticut troops mutinied while in camp near Morristown, and a brigade of the Pennsylvania line was called out to quell the disturbance.

but was with Some Difficulty Desperst but at
Night they all paraded and Marched to the
Barracks where my men was and about forty of
my Regt Joined them after talking some time
with them they all Disperst and Remained in
peace the night.

January 29. A fine pleasant morning
and at Roll Call I ordered fore of my Men
Whipt for attempting and Robbing a Corporal
for Informing the officers that they were a
turning out with their Arms, in the afternoon
I and Gen Varnum went to Providence from
thence I went to my fathers there tarried the
Night.

Jany. 30th, 1779. A pleasant morning
and after breakfast I set off for Providence but
could do no business with the Council of war
in the afternoon I set off for my own hous and
a violent Stormy time I had as it snow'd all
the way home I got to my own hous about
sunset found all well.

The fourth of January the next year the Pennsylvania troops mutinied, some blood was shed, and a serious state of affairs was averted
only by the prompt and firm action of General Wayne. A few
days later the New Jersey line cantoned at Pompton, N.J., mutinied,
and left the camp, closely pursued by General Howe (American),
who suppressed the revolt and executed some of the ringleaders.
May 6, 1782, another mutiny among the Connecticut troops occurred
near Fishkill, which was promptly surpressed. (Thatcher's " Military Journal," pp. 198, 246, 251, 310.)

January 31, 1779. it had Cleared off and was good Weather this morning I spent the Day in running about the Neighbourhood to day on busines and tarried at my own hous the Night following.

Febry. 1st, 1779. A fine pleasant morning after Breakfast I set of for Camp at Warren it Remained Exceeding Plesant over head but thaw'd So as to make it bad traviling I arrived in Camp by Sunset and found all well Col Peck [1] and Doctor Hagan [2] was at my Q^{rs}

[1] Probably William Peck (Conn.), Adjutant 17th Continental Infantry, 1st January, 1776; Brigade Major to General Spencer, 28th July, 1776; Major and Aide-de-Camp to General Spencer, 14th August, 1776, to January, 1778; served also as Colonel and Deputy Adjutant-General of Forces in Rhode Island, 20th May, 1777, until he resigned, about October, 1781. (Heitman's " Officers of the Continental Army.") See also Providence Town Papers, Nos. 1452, 2145.

[2] There was a Francis Hagan, of New Jersey, who was Hospital Physician and Surgeon, Oct. 6, 1780; he resigned the service May 25, 1781.

PART THREE.

A PORTION of this section of the diary has been lost, the first entry, which was apparently for the eighteenth of June, 1779, being incomplete,— it refers to the engagement at Charlestown Neck, South Carolina, on May 11, 1779, news of which had only then been received.

The part concludes with the fourteenth of August, 1779, when the regiment was encamped at Barbers' Heights, in North Kingstown, Rhode Island.

. . . Army being Defeted in an Action against Charlestown,[1] South Carolina, the Enemy was Pressing on to gain the town Gen[l] Lincon was in the Rear the Enemy was Repulsed and Retreated then Rallied Come on the Second time and was totally defeated thus Ends the Day with this Glorious News.

---

[1] In this engagement General Lincoln sustained a loss, according to Gordon (British), of killed and wounded, 146, besides 155 missing.

19th. Nothing Remarkable this Day.

June 20th, 1779. Fine weather and nothing remarkable untill Evening when we had the grand news of the Brittish armys being Entirely Defeted in georgia.

21st. Good weather, this Day I sent to Coxet [1] to divide the prize taken by the weasel and nothing Remarkable happens

June 22d, 1779. This day all the officers of my Regt and Colo Sherburnes met at a place called Pecks Rocks [2] where they had a grand Entertainment I did not attend my self with them, in the afternoon Recd an express from General Gates [3] Desiring me to attend head Quarters. I set off immediately, when I Come to Providence the Gen[l] informed me he was going to Remove my Regt to Boston neck and Coi Jackson's to Warren. I went to my Brother Whipples and tarried the night.

June 23, 1779. Left Providence this morning after waiting on the Gen[l] arrived at

---

[1] Acoxet, a part of Dartmouth, Mass., also spelled Coaksett. (See Plymouth Colony Records, Vol. IV., p. 65.)

[2] The place called Peck's Rocks is located at the mouth of the Warren River, nearly opposite Rumstick Point, in the town of Bristol, R.I. It was near here that the British forces landed when they made the attack on the towns of Warren and Bristol, May 25, 1778.

[3] Gen. Horatio Gates held command of the troops in Rhode Island from April to November, 1779.

Camp about ten oclock AM went to preparing for a move.

24th. This morning we packt up all our baggage and begun to Remove it to warren. I rode out into Swansey to Mr. Hills Tavern to take my leave of them. Returned and dined with Gen. Miller[1] then went to the camp and

---

[1] Gen. Nathan Miller was born in the town of Warren, R.I. (then Swansea, Mass.), March 20, 1743. He was the oldest son of Nathan and Patience (Turner) Miller, being sixth in line of descent from John Miller, one of the early settlers of Rehoboth, and fifth in line of descent from Capt. William Turner, who lost his life during Philip's War, while in command of a volunteer company at Turner's Falls. His paternal great-great-grandmother was Elizabeth, daughter of William Sabine, a Huguenot refugee of wealth and culture, whose name appeared upon the Rehoboth records as early as 1643. His grandfather, Samuel Miller, was a large landed proprietor, and was among the first in Warren to engage in ship building. The Miller family were prominent members of the social, political, and religious circles of their native town, and gave their name to one of its principal streets.

At the outbreak of the Revolution General Miller and his brother, William Turner Miller, at once embraced the cause of liberty, and throughout the war both labored diligently in defence of their country. In 1775 Nathan Miller was chosen Commissary to General Hopkins' troops. In 1777 he was appointed a recruiting officer. In 1778 he became a member of the Council of War. In the spring of this year, he, in connection with Le Baron Bradford, Samuel Pearce, Samuel Brown, and Cromwell Child fitted out the privateer sloop "General Stark," of fourteen guns, which captured two or more prizes, though eventually falling into the hands of the enemy. During the battle of Rhode Island he was in command of a regiment. In 1779, after having been advanced through various military grades, he was appointed Brigadier-General of the counties of Newport and Bristol. Throughout that and the following year he served on various committees. So arduous were his many duties

found a man there who had brought a load of the goods from our prize at Coxet the goods was at Kickemuit Bridg we went imeadetly to carting it to warren and at three o'clock all the tents was struck loaded into the waggons a little after four the Reg^t marched off the Ground went to Warren where they tarried the night in my Journal of the 22nd forgot to mention one Mellencully Accident which happend two young men of my Reg^t Benjamin Bird and

---

that in 1781 he decided to withdraw from public life, but at the request of the General Assembly reconsidered his determination, and in August of that year was placed in command of the flag-of-truce "Nancy" and proceeded to New York for the purpose of negotiating an exchange of prisoners. In 1782 he was chosen one of a committee to sell certain confiscated estates, and was also a member of the committee of ways and means. He continued his active participation in public affairs until his death, which occurred March 20, 1790.

General Miller represented Warren as a Deputy to the General Assembly for a period of nine years. In February, 1786, he was elected a delegate to the United States Congress, the Rev. James Manning, D.D., President of Rhode Island College, being his colleague.

With the French officers stationed in Rhode Island General Miller was on most intimate terms, his Huguenot blood forming a bond of union mutually agreeable. General Lafayette, while encamped at Warren, was his frequent guest, and a warm friendship existed between the two. General Miller was also greatly attached to Count Rochambeau, with whom he exchanged swords. The Rochambeau sword is a handsome rapier, the blade ornamented with gold and blue, while the hilt and guard are of silver. It is owned by a descendant of General Miller, and is a highly prized heirloom.

The personal appearance of General Miller was very striking, owing to his remarkable size. His weight was above three hun-

James Lobb were both drowned in Kickemuit
River the first men lost out of the Regt Since
the action on the Island — by Death

June 25th, 1779.   This morning I turnd
out by two o'clock and before four had all the
troops embarkt and on their passage.   I tarried
myself till after Breakfast then went on by
land in Company with Lt Jeruald [1] and his
wife to Providence as I was a member of a
Court Martial to set there by adjournment for
the trial of Col Vose [2] arrived in Providence

---

dred pounds. His boots were said to have held a bushel of corn
apiece, while four boys were easily buttoned into his vest.

The Marquis de Chastellux, in the narrative of his travels
through America, alludes to the great corpulency of the general,
and also to the remarkable size of his sister, Mrs. Burr, wife of the
landlord of the famous Warren hostelry, Burr's Tavern.

General Miller married his cousin, Rebekah Barton, daughter of
Samuel and Lillis (Turner) Barton, Jan. 8, 1764. She survived him
several years, dying Aug. 21, 1817. By this marriage there were
two children: a son, Caleb, who died in early youth, and a daughter,
Abigail, who married Charles Wheaton, of Providence.

The old Miller homestead is still standing in Warren, at the foot
of Miller street. Many years ago it passed from the Miller family into
stranger hands. Though somewhat decayed, it preserves its colonial appearance, and forms one of the most interesting of Warren's
ancient landmarks.

[1] Dutee Jerauld, recommended by General Washington and
appointed 2d Lieutenant of the Second Battalion raised by the
Colony of Rhode Island, October, 1776. (See Rhode Island Colonial Records, Vol. VII., p. 11.) Appointed 1st Lieutenant, February, 1777. (Same, Vol. VIII., p. 127.)

[2] " Head Quarters July 9th 1779 Field Officer Major Trescott
"The Genl Court Martial held the 2nd. June 1779 and Continued
by adjournment until the 6th July of which B Genl Starks was Pres-

half after nine but the president was gone into the Country and I Went to Johnston to see my family where I arrived by two oclock & found all well but was much unwell myself.

---

ent Col⁰ Joseph Vose Commander of the 4th Regiment from the State of Massachusetts Bay was Tryed for a Complaint Exhibited from a number of his officers for fraud for Taking a Quantaty of Rum Drawn for the Reg^t for his own use Sec^d. in Defrauding the United States of a Number of Shirts out Major Shipherdes Store at Albany thir^d. for Selling a Horse belonging to the United States to an Inhabitant Near Valley Forge 4th for Drawing pay for being on Command while on Furlough 5th for keeping the Taylors employed by the United States to work for the army and alowed extra Pay there for. at work for those of his famaly that did not belong to the Service 6th for Drawing pay for a Serjeants Doing Q^r Mafters duty and keeping all the mony But Seven Dollors & ½ p^r. Month in his own hands & Converting it to his own use 7th. for Sending home Blankits Drawn from the Store for the Regiment 8th for using Cloth Drawn for the Regiment to make his hired men Clothes 9th for Genl. UnGentlemanlike behavour to the officers of his Regiment. The Charges being Read to Col⁰ Vose he pleaded not Guilty the Court upon a Mature and full Consideration of the Respective Charges, and the Evidences for and against Col⁰ Vose and of oppinion on the first Charge that Col⁰. Vose was by no Means Justifyable in Taking the Rum which it appeared he did but on the Contrary is highly Repremandable yet in Consideration of the Trifelling Quantaty he Took and the Necessity he appears to be under for the Rum The Commissary not having any at that Time and his Charractor as an Officer acquit him of any Intintion of defrauding the Soldiers in this Instent on each and every other of the Charges the Court are of oppinion that they are not Supported & that Col⁰. Vose is not Guilty of any one of the Instinces of which he is Charged & there for acquit him & the Genl. Confirmes the Judgement of the Court, and orders Col⁰. Vose to be Relesed from his arrest & to Take Command of his Regiment. The Genl Court Martial of which B. Genl. Glovers is president is Desolved." — *Orderly Book, Headquarters, Providence.*

June 26, 1779. Clowdy and foggy after Breakfast went on to join my Reg^t. went to East Greenwich there Din'd. then went on to Barbers Hill ^{1} where I found the Reg^t Encampt when I had got to the Regt was all most Sick it being an exceeding hot Day and I had not been well for Several Days before Col. Greene Maj Flagg ^{2} were both at the Encampment when I came there.

June 27, 1779. I was in a shocking situation of health this morning, but got some better in the afternoon and Road to updike Newtown and Reconitered the Shore betwixt the encampment and the above said town then went to Maj^r Gardners there Drunk tea and Returned to the camp thus ends the day

June 28th. A clowdy Raw windy morning this being the day that the battle was at Monmoth ^{3} I prepaird and Entertainment for all

---

^{1} Barber's Height is a commanding eminence in North Kingstown two hundred feet above the sea level; from its highest point a view can be obtained of the whole lower bay (Narragansett) and for many miles off to sea.

^{2} Flagg, Ebenezer (R.I.), Captain 2d Rhode Island Regiment, 28th June to December, 1775; Captain 9th Continental Infantry, 1st January to 31st December, 1776; Captain 1st Rhode Island, 1st January, 1777; Major, 26th May, 1778; killed, 14th May, 1781, by Delancy's Tories in Westchester County, New York. (Heitman's "Officers of the Continental Army.")

^{3} The battle of Monmouth took place June 28, 1778; in this engagement Angell's Regiment bore a conspicuous part, being in the division commanded by General Lee.

the Officers of my Reg^t. and all Dind togeather there Came a brigg in from Sea this afternoon I orderd a piece of artillery down on the shore and brought her too. it proved to be a Brigg from Sandy Cruze bound to Providence with Rum and Sowering on board thus Ends the Day William Jacobs master of the abovesd Brigg.

June 19th, 1779. Clowdy Morning Capt Humphrey [1] a Sergt and four men was sent to Greenwich this morning at Sunrise on Busness. Nothing of Consequence happened this Day.

30th. This Day we had an Invitation to Dine with a Number of Gentlemen and ladies at one Mr Gardners who lived upon the farm that was Rooms.[2] I and Col Olney went,

---

[1] Humphrey, William (R.I.), Lieutenant of Varnum's Rhode Island Regiment, June, 1775; taken prisoner at Quebec, 31st December, 1775; 1st Lieutenant 2d Rhode Island, 1st January, 1777; Captain, 22d October, 1777; transferred to 1st Rhode Island, 1st January, 1781, and served to close of war. (Heitman's "Officers of the Continental Army.")

A journal of the expedition against Quebec, kept by him, is in the possession of his great-grandson, George Humphrey, Esq., of Providence, R.I.

[2] George Rome, "a gentleman of estate" and a merchant from England, came to Rhode Island in 1761, as the agent of the house of Halsey & Hopkins.

He resided in Newport winters, and in Narragansett summers. His estate was located on Boston Neck, in North Kingstown, and

and spent the Day very agreable being a very respectable company of the most principal Inhabitants for Several miles around.

July 1st, 1779. An Exceeding Raney

---

consisted of about seven hundred acres, "bounding easterly on the Narragansett Bay.

"The mansion house was highly finished and furnished. The beds were concealed from view in the wainscots — the rooms might be traversed throughout, and not a bed for the repose of the guests be seen.   .   .   .

" When the hour for retirement arrived, a servant would just give a touch to a spring in the ceiling and the visitor's bed, by means of a self-adjusting process, would protrude itself, as if by the effect of magic, ready prepared for the reception of its tenant."

His grounds were elegantly embellished, and he entertained with "sumptuous hospitality."

In the Stamp Act excitement he wrote a letter to a friend in Boston in which he reviled the Legislature, the Courts, and juries of the Colony, and charged general corruption therein. It aroused the most intense excitement.

He was summoned before the Legislature at its session in October, 1773, in South Kingstown, and questioned as to his expressions; but he evaded all the questions and was adjudged in contempt, and by order of the House was committed to the common gaol of South Kingstown, where he remained until the House rose. "After his release from prison, realizing the extent of popular feeling against him and fearing that it might work him still more bodily harm, he 'fled on board of the " Rose," man-of-war, then lying in the Narragansett bay.' "

His estates were later seized by the Colony, and at a session of the General Assembly, in October, 1775, a committee was appointed to sell at public auction all the effects of George Rome in possession of the State and pay the money into the State Treasury.

For Acts of the General Assembly relating to this affair, see Vol. XII., Rhode Island Colonial Records, pp. 376, 394, 421, 499, 520, 549. See also my "Esek Hopkins, Commander-in-Chief of the American Navy." p. 53.

morning with Thunder and Showers Lt Cook [1] of Col. Greenes Regt. Come from the Meroon frolick [2] last night and Tarried in Camp Breakfasted with me and after Dinner Set off for Greenwich where we arrived in the afternoon and after Drinking a glass of wine with the Governor [3] went on for my own hous where arrived by Sunset found all well.

2d. it Storming this Day I tarried at my own hous the Day and nothing Remarkable happened.

3d. Clear and pleasant I set off with Mr Stevens this morning for Providence Mr Luther went with his team to bring up Some Stores for me that the Weasel brought and nails for a barn I waited upon the Genl for liberty to tarry until the Court Martial Set which was on Monday this was Saturday the request was granted me after doing what business I had to do returned to my hous in Johnston by two o'clock Joseph

---

[1] Cooke, John (R.I.), Ensign 1st Rhode Island, 1st January, 1777; 2d Lieutenant, 1st June, 1778; Regimental Quartermaster,   , 1778, to   ; was in service May, 1780. (Heitman's "Officers of the Continental Army.")

[2] A hunting or fishing trip, or excursion, in Southern United States, to camp out after the manner of the West Indian Maroons; a pleasure excursion of some duration, with provisions for living in camp. "Marooning Cases" are frequently mentioned in old inventories. See Prov. Probate Records, Wills, No. 11, p. 38.

[3] William Greene, Jr., Governor from May, 1778, to May, 1786, who lived near East Greenwich.

Thrasher [1] a deserter from my Regt. was taken near Providence Confined in the Main guard yesterday by Capt Joab Sweeting [2] an inhabitant.

July 4th, 1779. fine weather this being Sunday I tarried at home untill after noon then went to Meeting at Samuel Angell's returned with a number of ladies and Spent the afternoon very agreable.

July 5th. Clear and pleasant morning my people begun this morning to make preparations to raise a barn I went to Providence to attend the Court Martial but it being a day for the Selebrating our Independence the Court stood adjourned until tomorrow morning Six oclock So I returned home and attended on the Raising of my Barn which was rais'd in the Afternoon without Aney Accident happening.

July 6th, 1779. I set off By Sunrise this morning for Providence to attend the Court which did not meet untill near nine oclock when we proceeded to business and finished before

---

[1] Joseph Thrasher, of Capt. William Tew's Company.

[2] Job Sweeting, appointed Dec. 24, 1774, with others, a committee for resisting the Act of the British Parliament imposing a duty on tea, and for otherwise raising a revenue in the American Colonies.

February, 1776, appointed, with others, a committee to procure as much gold and silver coin as they can for the operations in Canada. He does not appear to have been engaged in any military service. Many references to him are in Providence Town Papers.

Sunset as Genl Glovers Brigade was ordered to move it became necessary for the trial to be ended as soon as possible therefore the Court set in the Afternoon, which is not Agreable to the Articles of war Except in cases of Necessity like this. this day we recd the news of the death of Capt Joseph Olney of North Providence, who departed this life this morning very Sudden just before day. his wife observed him to fetch a Sigh and a groan She spoke to him but he did not answer her, and died imeadietley without speaking another word I returned to my own hous this Evening.

July 7th, 1779. This day I expected to have gone to Boston Neck to join the Regt. but my wife had a mind to go to see her mother so after Dinner I and my wife set off for her mothers and I returned in the Evening in order to sett off for the Camp Early in the morning.

July 8th. This morning I got up very Early in order to set off on my journey for the Camp but my horse had run away and took me all the forenoon to look for him in the afternoon I set off for Camp went to Green-wich there Col. Greene Desired me to tarry with him until next day and he and Major Flagg would both go with me. I tarried and

between two and three o'clock in the morning
we were allarmed by the firing of small arms
below towards New Town [1] on which the Allarm
Guns were fird at New Town and warwick.

9th. I immediately on the Allarm set off
for Camp arrived at New Town before Sunrise
on my way there mett some Militia who informed me that there was three Boats with
about one Hundred men landed at Quonset [2]
above new town & Plundered John Dyer's
Hous of Some Small matter of goods he himself crept out on the Rough (roof) of the hous
and made his Escape. then I tarried at Newtown untill Ensign Pratt [3] Returned as he was
gone to Col Dyers to see what intelligence he
could get but he returned with no more than I
had heard before we then Set off for Camp it
had rained Considerable in the morning, and
imeaditely set in to raining Exceeding hard by
which means I got as wet as water would make
me by the time I got to the Camp it Cleared off
by noon nothing more Remarkable happened.

---

[1] Updike's New-town, now Wickford.

[2] Quonset Point or Seconiquonset Point (see Harris Map State
of Rhode Island, 1795), to the north-east of the village of Wickford,
in North Kingstown. The Rhode Island State Militia camp-grounds
are located there.

[3] William Pratt appointed Ensign by General Assembly of Rhode
Island, June, 1780, commission to date from May 1, 1779. (Rhode
Island Colonial Records, Vol. IX., p. 90.)

10th. This Day being pleasant I with five or six of my officers went to Col Sands[1] Tower Hill[2] to dine with him and spent the day I forgot to mention that on the 8th Recd the Disagreeable News of the Enemys having possession of new Haven[3] we Daily have intelligence from them Yesterday we heard that they had burnt fairfield and to Day it was Confirmd we further heard that they were of against New London.[4]

July 11th, 1779. This Day I went on Dutch Island[5] Returned by Two oclock and

---

[1] Ray Sands lived at Tower Hill and in 1775 was appointed Postmaster at the office there established. In October of that year he was chosen Captain of the Third Company in South Kingstown, and again in 1776. In July, 1776, he was chosen Major of the Second Regiment of Militia in Kings County, holding this position for a few months, when he was advanced to the position of Colonel, "in the room of Samuel Seagar, who is gone to sea."

Colonel Sands was stationed at Boston Neck and Point Judith in December, 1776, in command of detachments sent there for guard duty. At the March session of the General Assembly, 1777, it was made known that the election of Sands in place of Seagar was to the office of Lieutenant-Colonel instead of Colonel, the Secretary having erroneously made the record and issued a commission. This mistake made necessary several changes, all of which may be found explained in Rhode Island Colonial Records, Vol. 8, pp. 179, 180.

[2] To the south-west of Barbers Heights and east of Boston Neck, 178 feet above tide water.

[3] These were the raids made by Tryon against the towns on the Connecticut coast.

[4] New London was spared an attack, the raiders being called to New York on account of the Stony Point engagement.

[5] Dutch Island lies to the south of Barbers Heights, and against the western shores of Conanicut Island.

it soon Set in to Storming thus Ended the
Day.

12th.   Last Night was as Stormy a Night
perhaps as Ever Known with rain wind and
Thunder numbers of the Marques and tents
blow Down and the greatest part of the troops
was as wet as the water would make them it
Cleared off this Day by a little after 12 oclock.
a Court Martial [1] Set at Mr. Moreys in Newtown to try two Deserters from my Regt John
Deruce and Joseph Thrasher a further Confir-
mation Come this Day of the Enemy's burning
fairfield.

13th.   Nothing Remarkable this day

14th.   The Same to Day as yesterday

July 15th, 1779.   This Day Recd news
that there was nothing in the Report of the
Action at Charlestown South Carolina but
think it all most impossible that Lying Could
be Carried to such a pitch I went to Newtown
Major Thayer to Warren.

---

[1] "At a Brigade Court Martial held at Updike Newtown on the
12th Instant (July 12 1779) of which Lt. Colo Olney was Presidt
John Deruse of Colo. Angills Regiment was Tryed for Desersion to
the Enemy and Carrying with him a Guard Boat — The Prisoner
being Brought Before the Court Pleads Guilty The Court therefore
Sentence him To Suffer Death — The Genl. approves the Sentence
of the Court — Joseph Thrasher of Colo. Angells Regiment Tryed at
the above Court for Desertion found Guilty and Sentenced to Re-
ceve one hundred lashes on his Bare Back — The Genl. approves
the Sentence and Orders the punishment inflicted immeadiately."

16th. Clear Cold and windy weather I Col Houg( ) and Capt. Allen[1] went round what is called Boston Neck below where we lay on Barbers Hights Returned and found Col Greene in Camp this Evening Major Thayer Returned from Warren

July 17th, 1779. Clowdy and Exceeding Windy and Cold but nothing happened extraordinary

18th Nothing Remarkable this day

19th. This Evening we Read a hand bill from Providence that General Wayne with 1200 of the light troops had taken the Brittish fort on Stoney Point[2] at Kings ferry on North River he took the fort on Surprise Carri'd it with the loss of four men killed and Eleven wounded, the garrison Consisted of five hundred Brittish troops who were all killd and made prisoners to a man it is said 100 of them were killed and wounded.

---

[1] Allen, William (R.I.), 1st Lieutenant 11th Continental Infantry, 1st January to 31st December, 1776; 1st Lieutenant 2d Rhode Island, 1st January, 1777; Captain 13th January, 1777; transferred to 1st Rhode Island, 1st January, 1781; Brevet-Major 30th September, 1783; served to 3d November, 1783. (Heitman's "Officers of the Continental Army.")

[2] Captured by Gen. Anthony Wayne, July 16, 1779; but after holding the Point for three days, "the works were all destroyed, and the garrisons with the cannon and stores withdrawn into the Highlands." It required a greater force to hold it than could be spared from the army.

July 20, 1779. Nothing Remarkable this Day.

21st. This day we had a fu-de-joy on the occation of Stoney point fort being taken by firing thirteen peaces of Cannon I with a number of gentlemen Dind with Peter Phillips Esqr [1] thus ends the day.

July 22d, 1779. Nothing Remarkable this Day.

23d. This morning a fleet appeared off point Judath of 37 sail and by night were all in the harbor of Newport Except one or two

24th. This morning I sent Lt Thomas Waterman an Express to head Q^{rs} with the returns of my Reg^t and a number of letters and in the afternoon had the Mortification to finde that Two thirds of the Serg^{ts} in the Reg^t had conspired togeather and ript the bindings of their hatts Contrary to orders I issued an

---

[1] Peter Phillips was a Deputy to the General Assembly of Rhode Island in May, 1772, 1773, 1774. He was appointed on a committee to make enumeration of the inhabitants of the colony in 1774; an Assistant in May, 1775. In 1775 he was appointed Commissary of the Army of Observation and held commission as Deputy Commissary under Trumbull for some years thereafter. In 1776, 1779, and 1780 he was an Assistant and appointed one of a committee to manage confiscated estates. He later held the position of Justice of the Superior Court for several years. A letter from Jonathan Trumbull, dated Hartford, Jan. 20, 1777, to Capt. Asa Waterman, says: "You will find Mr. Phillips an exceedingly good man, lend him any assistance in your power."

order for them to put them on by next morning by guard mounting or they should be reduced to the ranks with out the formality of a
Court Martial and tried for a willful Disobedience of orders.

25th July, 1779. This morning by
Eight oclock the Sergt[s] had all their bindings
on in the afternoon yesterday I recd a muti-
nious paper from one of the Soldiers wrote by
one Hazzard and brought by one Twitchel and
last Evening Two Deserters John Deruce and
Robert Albro [1] both made their Escape from
the Q[r] Guard Deruce was in Irons and under
Sentence of death, he is supposed to have
been taken out of his irons by one Fowler who
was confin'd with him. I set out for to see
the Genl at providence on business this afternoon half past 4 oclock went to my own hous
tarried the night.

26th July. A Raney morning after breakfast went off for providence Din'd with Gov-
ernour Bowen [2] finished my business and
return'd to Camp before nine o'clock in the
evening had news to day of the Enemy going
up North River with all their force.

---

[1] Robert Albro, of Capt. William Tew's Company. (See my
" Revolutionary Defences in Rhode Island," p. 126.)

[2] Jabez Bowen, Deputy-Governor of Rhode Island from May,
1778, to May, 1780, and from May, 1781, to May, 1786.

July 27th, 1779. Clowdy and wet morning after breakfast I went a fishing the Day Eanded with nothing remarkable happening.

July 28th, 1779. This morning half after Seven oclock I set off in a boat with five men for warren arrivd there by half after two in the afternoon Dined at Mr Luthers and Tarried there that night.

July 29th. This morning it Rained the wind was Northeast I should have Set off for the Camp, had the Boat Returned from providence which I sent up the evening before, and I got my busness done but the boat did not return till near night which obliged me to Stay in warren this night.

30th. This morning I got up before sunrise Went up to where the Artillery was encampt there staid and breakfasted then return'd to warren but the wind shifting from N. E to S W could not set off untill the tide turn'd as the wind was ahead about 9 o'clock set sail beat out of warren River gaind the Bay but the tide running against the wind, and the wind blowing very heavy Caus't so great a Swell that the Spray of the See broke over us so that we Should soon ben as wet as water would make us I ordered the boat about and Run back to warren landed on Barrington Shore where I fell in Company with Capt Tew went home with him and Staid the afternoon and night with him as the wind Continued to blow hard.

July the 31st and last, 1779. After Breakfasting at Capt Tew went to warren there Recd the Disagreeable news of my Reg^t mutinying on which I set off to try to reach the western shore though the wind was a head we beat out of warren river Stood over to Warwick neck [1] and after trying to beat Down to Barbers hights, was obliged to put away for Greenwich harbor there Left my boat and men got a hors and set off for Camp arriv'd there by Eight o'clock found all in peace on my way met Genl Stark and a number of other Gentlemen who had been down to the Regt at the Request of Gen Gates, and ordered the Regt to parade and march by the Column they all Recd the genl pardon except George Millamen who was ordered to be Sent prisoner in irons to providence and was imeadetly sent off.

August the 1st, 1779. A Raney morning and Continued Storming the greatest part of the Day but nothing Remarkable happened.

---

[1] Here was an important military post, and a garrison was maintained during the years of the war. For a more particular account see my "Revolutionary Defences in Rhode Island."

August 2d. Clowdy and raw after Breakfast I Col. Olney Capt Hughes Lt Sayls all Set off for Providence went as far as Greenwich there heard that the Council of War was upon busness and could not attend to do the busness we were a going upon. So I and Lt Sayls went on Lt Col. Olney and Capt Hughes tarried to dine in greenwich I parted with Lt Sayls at Greens Bridg^1 I come home and tarrid at my own hous

August 3d, 1779. This morning was very Raney but held up a little before noon and I went to Catch my hors to go to Providence but he broke out of the pasture into the woods and I was not able to catch him till near the middle of the afternoon then went to Providence found it necessary for me to be in Camp by the next morning So set off imeadetly went to greenwich There tarried the night.

4th August. Left Greenwich this evening at day break arrived in Camp [   ] the sun an hour high. Sent Major Thayer off

---

^{1} This is sometimes called Major Greene's Bridge, and is referred to in records as "ye bridge called Major Greene's bridge." In May, 1771, the town of Warwick petitioned the General Assembly of Rhode Island to grant a lottery to repair this bridge, it having been carried away by a freshet. It is described in the petition as over the Pawtucket River, about six miles above the falls. The present bridge at Pontiac, R.I., serves to mark approximately its location.

with Capt Coggeshall Olney and Ensign
Wheaton [1] for Providence as Evidence against
George Milliman who was to be tried this day
for Mutiny in the afternoon there Come a
man to my Marquee who informed me that he
belonged to the galley which lay below Providence and had been out by Block Island in the
Galleys boat and taken three fisherman boats
who were all on their way to Providence and
had Calld at the Shore to give me intelligence
I went and [   ] one of the prisoners who informed me that the Tory fleet intended to
Come off a plundering on point Judath this
night or tomorrow night   Thus ends the
Day.

5th August, 1779.   Last night I Rec'd
an Express from the Adj^t. General that the
Court to try Millamen wanted Eight non com-
missioned officers and Soldiers of my Regt as
Evidences which I sent off about midnight this
was a Clear and pleasant morning and the
Tory's Did not trouble us last Night as we had
Reason to Expect by the acc^t Rec'd the Even-

---

[1] Joseph Wheaton, appointed Ensign by General Assembly of
Rhode Island, June, 1780, commission to date from May 1, 1779.

"General Sullivan's Orderly Book, Headquarters, Providence,
March 3 1779," contains this entry:

"Lieut. Joseph Wheaton (of Lieutenant-Colonel Peabody's State
Regiment) is appointed Ensign in Col. Israel Angells Continental
Regiment."

ing before   I tarrid in Camp till after Dinner
then Rode all round the neck called Boston
neck Returned to Camp before Sun Set.

6th August, 1779. Early this morning
Major Gardner Come to Camp and brought
news that our fleet that went down to the Eastward to penobscot had landed their Land
forces and taken the Brittish Batteries at the
same time the fleet had block't in their shipping
and the enemy had Sunk all their Ships and
Surrendered themselves prisoners to the amount
of Two thousand men Maj^r Thayer { Returned
to Camp from Providence last night about ten
o'clock nothing remarkable happened till in
the evening there came a Deserter from off
Conanicutt Island from the enemy who Swam
over to Dutch Island from thence to the neck,
he was so weak when he landed that he could
not stand for Some time having Swam near
three miles [all this days journal to the mark{
happened the morning before but was omitted
being Entered through mistake] This day
ended with nothing More remarkable than
what has been related.

August 7th, 1779. Clowdy morning
and begun to rain and rained very hard and
continued raining all the Day and was as Rainy a
night as was Ever known with very hard thunder.

8th. A Raney morning and perhaps never more rain fell in one night than there did last night it cleared off to day Lt Col. Olney Com to Camp to day nothing remarkable happened during the Day.

August 9th, 1779. Clowdy and foggy this morning Col Olney Set off for providence to attend the Court Martial the fogg broke away it was a fine day I Spent part of this day a fishing at night we Recd news of Col Talbutts having taken Stanton Hazzard[1] the Tory pirat from Rhode Island and Carried him into Newlondon

10th. Nothing Remarkable this day.

11th. Nothing remarkable.

August 12th, 1779. Continues the Same as yesterday.

13th. Peace and Quietness.

14th. This Day sent a boat to Point judath for a wounded man [   ] Jacksons Reg^t to carry him to [   ] his father havin come after him living in Dighton Showering wet weather Eand this journal.

---

[1] For portrait see "The Hazard Family of Rhode Island, 1635–1894," by Caroline E. Robinson, also genealogical account.

The historical statements in this volume relating to Stanton Hazard are critically considered by Sidney S. Rider, A.M., in "Book Notes," Vol. XIII., No. 10, where is also a letter regarding this event, from Silas Talbot to General Gates.

PART FOUR.

THE period covered by this part of the
diary is from October 3, 1779, to December 13, 1779.

During this time the Rhode Island Regiment
was encamped on Barbers Height, in North
Kingstown, in Rhode Island, until after the
evacuation of Newport by the British, when all
the Continental troops in Rhode Island were
ordered to the westward.

Before taking up the march, however, Colonel
Angell spent a short time with his family at
home, and joined his regiment at Danbury,
Conn., from which place the regiment marched
to Morristown, New Jersey. The diary is
prefaced as follows :

A Journal Continued from 2nd of October 1779

Encamped on Barbers Hights North kingstown

Eanded 13th December

In Morristown Mountains

October 3d, 1779.   Plesant weather and

Nothing Remarkable happend Except the Stopping of two Small Sloops in Newtown loaded with Rum Sugar and wine, bound to Connecticutt, and as there was an Embargo laid on those articals, and not to be Carried out of the State, it was my Duty to Stop them, untill they had a pass from that authority that past the non Exportation act, I wrote a letter to the Governor, Sent it by one of the Gentlemen.

Octr. 4th. Warm and plesant weather, the Gentlemen I Sent to the Governor Returned with a permit from govenor, or rather a Recommen for them to pass on in their voige, this afternoon I was obliged to Stop a Sloop going from this port to Seaconk with twelve thousand weight of Chease, but the Gentleman produced an order from the board of war in boston to purchase Chease for the Navey, on which I let him proceed on with Said Chease, Ebenezer West[1] Formily a Lieu-

---

[1] Ebenezer West was chosen Ensign of the 2d Rhode Island Battalion, October, 1776. Of this battalion Israel Angell was Lieutenant-Colonel. (Rhode Island Colonial Records, Vol. VIII., p. 11.)

In February, 1777, West was chosen 1st Lieutenant in the same battalion, Israel Angell being advanced to the rank of Colonel. (Rhode Island Colonial Records, Vol. VIII., p. 126.) Heitman gives his military record as follows: Ensign 11th Continental Infantry, 1st January to 31st December, 1776; 1st Lieutenant 2d Rhode Island, 11th February, 1777; cashiered 9th July, 1778.

tenant in my Reg^t. Came to Camp this Evening to See his two Sones in my Reg^t.

October 5th, 1779. A Stormy morning, with the wind Northeast, and had Raind, the [ ]ratist part of the Night, and Continued Storming the whole Day

October 6th, 1779. A Clowdy weet morning. I had an Invitation to dine with Govenor Bradford, General Varnum and Col Thomas Potter [1] and a number of Gentlemen of the Superior Court at Little Rest.[2] I Col. Olney Capt Coggeshall Olney Capt Stephen Olney. Set off and dind with them and Returnd in the Evening, and perhaps it never raind much harder, we received News of Count

---

[1] Col. Thomas Potter, chosen Lieutenant-Colonel of the 2d Regiment of Militia in Kings County, December, 1776. In March, 1777, his appointment was revoked for the reason that it had been made by mistake; at the same time he was dismissed from service as Major, the time of the enlistment of the regiment to which he was appointed having expired. (Rhode Island Colonial Records, Vol. VIII., p. 180.)

At the March session of the General Assembly, 1777, he was appointed to represent South Kingstown on a committee for numbering all persons able to bear arms. In August of the same year he was appointed one of the recruiting officers for South Kingstown. (Rhode Island Colonial Records, Vol. VIII., p. 180.)

In May, 1779, he was chosen Colonel of the 3d Regiment of Militia, in the County of Kings. Probably the same Thomas Potter who was 1st Lieutenant of the Independent Company in South Kingstown, called the Kingstown Reds, in 1776.

[2] Little Rest Hill, in South Kingstown, where the Courts were held.

De Estaing being at georgia, and had landed
five thousand troops the 10th Sept

Octr. 7th, 1779. This morning it cleard
off, and after Breakfast I and Doctor Tenny
Set off for greenwich Dind there, and after
finishing my busness, went to Judg Northupts,[1]
for Shoes for my Reg[t]. from thence to Camp.
they informd me in Camp, that there had
been three large Ships Seen off, without block
Island but before night Disapeard

Octr. 8th, 1779. Cold and Windy I Sent
a boat to warren this Day.

In the Afternoon we Rec[d]. a report that
Count DEstaing was at Sandy Hook, and had
taken all the Brittish Shippen and men in
Georgia, and that there was one hundred and
fifty Sail Comming Down the Sound from New
York, Doctor Tenny[2] Come from Greenwich
this Evening and brought me a letter from
Col°. Ward[3] that the plan of the Barracks was

---

[1] John Northup, one of the Justices of the Court of Common
Pleas for Kings County, R.I. He was one of the Committee of
Safety, a member of the General Assembly, and actively engaged in
the affairs of the State during the war.

[2] Tenney, Samuel (R.I.), Surgeon's Mate of Gridley's Regiment,
Massachusetts Artillery, June to December, 1775; Surgeon 11th
Continental Infantry, 1st January to 31st December, 1776; Sur-
geon 2d Rhode Island, 1st January, 1777; transferred to 1st Rhode
Island, 1st January, 1781, and served to close of war. (Died 6th
February, 1816.) (Heitman's " Officers of the Continental Army.")

[3] Lieutenant-Colonel Samuel Ward (born Nov. 17, 1756; died

Come and Desired me to Come up to greenwich as Soon as possible.   Thus Eand the day

9th October, 1779. A plesant Morning
and after breakfast I and Col. Olney Set off
for greenwich to Consult on building the barracks, but Col°. Greene was unwell and Could
not attend, after we had been at Greenwich, I
went to Col° Greens Dind with him, then went
to my own hous found all well.

Octr. 10th, 1779. This morning after
breakfast Set off for Providence to See the
General, Concerning the barracks from thence
up into Wainscott to my fathers, from thence
home where I arrived by 9 °Clock

Octr. 11th, 1779. This morning after
breakfast I set off for Camp when I come to
Greenwich heard that there was A fleet got into
Rhode Island from New York, when I Come
to Camp found there had 57 Sail arrivd, among
which were 34 Ship, they appeard to be all
Empty, two of the privateer boats boarded one
of the vessels the men imeadetly ran down into
the hold, but before they Could git her away,
Come two barges and they were forst to
Leave her, the muster Master Come to Camp

Aug. 16, 1832) of the 1st Rhode Island Regiment.   He was retired
when the two Rhode Island regiments were consolidated.   He commanded a battalion of colored troops at the Battle of Rhode Island,
August, 1778.   A portrait is in Stone's " French Allies," opp. p. 86.

with me and Capt Hughes. Thus Eands the
Day —

Octr. 12th, 1779. This Morning after
breakfast my Reg^t was Mustered and I Set off
with the mustermaster and Major Thayer for
Greenwich where I expected to meet the General from Providence, but he did not Come,
and after Dining with the Governor, I Returned
to Camp Maj^r Thayer went on for providence.

October 13th, 1779. Clowdy weet morning, as it had Raind the greatest part of the
night past. Lt Col° Olney went off for providence this morning after breakfast, in the
afternoon I Sent a boat to Reconiter along
Connanicutt to see what discoveries they Could
make the people landed below Dutch Island
and none come to molest them, then they
landed above and went Near half a Cross the
Island Drove down Some horses with a view of
bringing Some of them off, but the Enemy
fired on them with a field peace, and imeadetly
Sent a party of light troops, which obliged them
to Come off without aney of the horses, they
Rowed along up the island — keepeing in with
the Shore, the Enemy pursued and begun a fire,
which was Returnd by the boats Crew but at
Such a distance that no Execution was done on
Either Side, there was imeadetly another party

of the Enemy Come up the Island of Near 100 men, but our people Come off with their boat and thus they had a march of Six or Seven miles for nothing, I Rec^d an Express from General Gates, Desiring me to keep a good look out, and give him the Earliest information of any movement of the Enemy, the Express informed me of an accident that befell one of my men who Was Sent after one Clefford a Deserter. Serj^t Chaffe,[1] and John Gould were Sent to take S^d Clefford, they took a boy an Inhabitant with them to show them the hous. they knocked at the Door but Could not be Admitted Enterence, they imeadetly broke open the Door, this Clefford run up Stairs, Goold followed him Clefford fird upon Gould with a pistol, the boy that was with them run off Screeming. Chaffe followed as is reported, in the morning Goolds hat was found in the hous with a ball fired through it but gould was not found when the Express Came away. Chaffe was gone to the General to know what further to Do. Thus Eands the Day.

October 14th, 1779. This Day we Rec^d. Several accounts Concerning Goulds being wounded or killd, but before night we heard he

---

[1] Probably Sergeant Noah Chaffee, of Capt. Coggeshall Olney's Company.

had got to providence, and at Night Major
Thayer Returnd and brought the news of Chaf-
fey and Gould Returning. Gould had Rec^d a
ball in his head as we had heard, but not to
break his Skull, Maj^r Thayer allso informd me
that we were under Marching orders, and
brought an order from the General to me for to
Call in all my out Commands, Lt Col Olney
Returned from providence this Evening. thus
Eand the Day.

October 15th, 1779. Clowdy and Cold
with a high wind from the Northeast, Lt.
Macomber[1] and Ensign Roggers[2] with a party
of men landed on Connanicutt last night, and
went over all the upper part of the Island, but
Could not take aney of the Inhabitants Except
Old men and women, without it was one
Hegron whome they brought off, we have

---

[1] Macomber, Ebenezer (R. I.), 1st Lieutenant of Richmond's
Rhode Island Regiment, 19th August to November, 1776; 1st Lieutenant of Tallman's Rhode Island State Regiment, 12th December,
1776; 1st Lieutenant 2d Rhode Island, 12th June, 1777; transferred
to 1st Rhode Island, 1st January, 1781; Captain, 17th March, 1782,
and served to 17th March, 1783. (Died 5th April, 1829.) (Heitman's "Officers of the Continental Army.")

[2] Rogers, John (R. I.), Ensign 2d Rhode Island, 1st May, 1779;
wounded at Connecticut Farms, 23d June, 1780; transferred to 1st
Rhode Island, 1st January, 1781; Lieutenant, August, 1781, and
served to close of war; Military Storekeeper United States Army,
9th March, 1819; honorably discharged 1st June, 1821. (Heitman's "Officers of the Continental Army.")

been Employed the Day in making Every preparation for marching

October 16th, 1779. This morning was windy and Cold as had ben before, one Mr Cole an inhabitant Come with a Complaint to me this morning that he had ben Abused by two of my Soldiers the night past, by their laying Violent hands on him throwing him down, and falling upon him the Regiment was imeadetly paraded and the Villins found and Confind, a Court Orderd to try them, and were both trid one of them ordered to be whipt one hundred lashes, viz, John Thomas, the other Daniel barney [1] a Corprol, was Reduced and floggd fifty Stripes —

October 17th, 1779. This day was very fine weather I was Exceeding busily employed all the forepard of the Day with pay abstracts, for both Continental and State, and after finishing my busness, went with Col° Olney and Major Thayer to dine with Col° John Gardner, there was a Ship of 28 or 30 guns, a brigg of 16 went into Newport Harbour and a Schoner Supposed to be a prize to the brigg one of the brittis Friggats went up the river towards the Eand of Conanicut thus eands the Day.

---

[1] Daniel Barney, formerly private in Capt. William Humphrey's Company.

18th October, 1779. No movements of the Enemy this Day to be discovered Major Thayer Capt. Hughes, and Lt Sayles — all went to providence this Day, Hews and Sayles went in the Morning Major Thayer went after Dinner with me as far as the ten rod road,[1] Where Col° Dyers Reg^t of Militia met for a review, as this Day was a Day that the Militia were mustered in every County in the State I returned to Camp in the Evening.

19th October. Nothing Remarkable happened this Day, a forty Gun Ship went up the River towards the upper Eand of Connanicut

October 20th, 1779. This Day I Sent a boat to Reconiter Connanicut, to See what Discoveries was to be made Ensign wheaton went in the boat, and brought off one Jonathan Greene a very Sincible young man who lived within the lines, who informed us that the Enemy was a going to avacuate the Island, had got all their heavey baggage and Cannon on

---

[1] The ten-rod road is a well-known highway in North Kingstown. It derives its name from being originally laid out ten rods wide, but since its original lay-out it has shrunk considerably in width, for abutting owners have been unable to resist the temptation to extend front walls and fences, and what was once a part of the common highway is now included in the front yards of abutters.

The road was laid out from Updike's Newtown (Wickford) westerly through the town of Exeter into Voluntown, Conn.

board, had burnt their platt forms in the North
battry, I saw the Smoak yesterday but forgot to
mention it Imeadetly Sent an Express to General Gates, by the movement of the Enemys
Ships it was thought they were a going, this
Evening.

21st Octr. 1799. The Enemys Ships
Remain in their former position, this Day Col
Olney Set off for Providence being So lame
as to be unfit for Duty, but meeting the General, who informed him that the Reg^t. would
go on the Island before they Marched to the
westward, he Sent back his Servant went to
providence, the Genl. Stark Come to the
Camp just before Sun Set, there was a very
heavey firing off at Sea this Afternoon, another was a brigg lay off point judath[1] firing
Signal Gunns till Dark there was a Great number of the Inhabitants in Camp this Day

October 22nd, 1779. This Day being
the Day that we defeated the Hessians at Red
banks in 1777, the officers of the Regiment
provided a Dinner and all Dind togeather,
with a great number of the Inhabitants, as
there was Some hundreds of people out of the
Country, on the hill looking out to See the
fleet go off but the wind not being fair pre-

---

[1] Point Judith, at the entrance to Narragansett Bay.

vented their Sailing, they Continued burning the platforms in their forts, and Some hay they had on Conanicut, yesterday they Set the light hous [1] on fire about Eleven °Clock, though I forgot to mention it in my journal the troops burned the Effigy of Count Dunop this Day and raised a liberty pole near fore Score feet high.

October the 23rd, 1779. A Strong South Wind this Day and the fleet Remained the Same as Yesterday, and the hill all Covered with people Looking out to See the fleet Sail

October 24th. Cloudy and weet, with the wind Northerly, there appeard a great Movement among the fleet, this morning but the wind Soon Died away and begun to weet, Stephen Phillips and Thomas Hearrendeen,[2] two Villins Deserted from my Reg^t. last Evening, and was Sent after this Morning: a great multitude of the Inhabitants Assembled here this Day to See the fleet go off their Signal Gun was fired and the fleet made preparation for Sailing but the wind died away and they remained at their Station, I sent a boat to Conanicut, and two of the Inhabitants Come

---

[1] Beaver Tail Lighthouse, at the southern end of Conanicut Island.

[2] Thomas Herenden, of Capt. Coggeshall Olney's Co.

off, who informd us that they Enemy was to have saild to Day, had the wind admited of it, in the afternoon there was a heavy Cannonade up the Sound, and before Night there Came five Ships Two briggs and one Schooner out of the Sound and went into Newport harbour

October 25th, 1779. A fine Plesant Morning and the fleet Remains the Same as yesterday, about the middle of the Day the Enemy begun to burn their Barracks and great movements was Seen among them, there was a great number of people in Camp to See the fleet Sail. among the Crowd was Governor Greens lady and daughter, the Britans was busy in Imbarking all the afternoon by Sunset was all on board, and the fleet Set Sail just after Sunset before Eleven °Clock in the evening was all without the light hous and we making preparation to take posession of the town [1] ──

October 26th, 1779. This morning at four o Clock all the troops paraded and marched for Roome point [2] Where they were to Embark on board their boats, the wind being very high and a Great Swell in the bay I Expected the boats would all have ben lost

---

[1] Newport, R.I.

[2] Romes Point is north of Barber's Height, at the entrance to Bissels Cove, in North Kingstown. It lies nearly opposite the north end of Conanicut Island.

with the men in them but With Great Difficulty the boats got to Conanicut, where two of them filld and were wrackt, in deed they were all nearly full of water when they Landed. I my Self was in a large boat with a deck more than half her length, and it was with great Difficulty that we kept the boat above water, untill we turnd the North Eand of Conanicut, — then we run nearly before the wind, and arrivd in Newport harbour half past Eight °Clock in the morning but the regiment marched on Conanicut to the ferry where I provided boats to bring the Same off and all Got Safe into the town before Night; the Shops was all Shut. and ordered to be kept So after the General Come in. the Inhabitants flockt in in great multitudes. Thus Eands this Day[1]

October 27th, 1779. A fine plesant Morning, and Continued So the day. I Spent this Day in Reconitering the Town, and works which was destroyed by the Enemy. and Sending to get over the Remainder of my baggage.

October 28th. a Clear plesant morning but Cool, after breakfast I road with the General Round all the Enemy Lines where I Saw

---

[1] The date of the evacuation of Newport is erroneously stated by Stone, in his " French Allies," as occurring on the 27th.

Some of the Beautifullest works[1] that I Ever Saw in my life, all my Camp equipage arrived this afternoon

October 29th, 1779. A plesant Day and Nothing Remarkable happend this Day: I was the Officer of the Day.

30th. Remarkable warm and Plesant, Nothing Remarkable happend this Day. I dind with General Stark

31st. Plesant Weather, this Morning I took my boat and went over to Conanicut there Reconiterd the Island viewd the forts Which the enemy had built found them Strong but Small, after Dining with Col° Levingston Returnd to Newport thus Eands the Month and Day,

November 1st, 1779. fine plesant weather for the Season, Nothing Remarkable happened this Day ——

2nd. Cold this morning and raind a little, wind very high, at north, I was the officer of the Day went to Brintons neck [2] viewed the Sod and Turf prepaird there by the brittish troops to burn in lieu of wood, there was two

---

[1] A detailed account of the fortifications in and around Newport may be found in my "Revolutionary Defences in Rhode Island."

[2] Brenton's Neck, the present neck of land which terminates at Fort Adams, Newport, R.I.

Sorts, one Cut in Strips out of a bog Swamp. the others was dug out of a pond place, workt the Same as morter, then made into three Squair peaces about one foot long Laid on the ground in rows and dryed then Set up on eand four togeather and one a top of them, after that they were pilld in roos from whence they were taken and Carted Some Distance and there Corded up in rows to Stand till they were wanted for use. the Day Eanded with nothing Remarkable

November 3rd, 1779. Cold raw and uncomfortable this morning Col° Greens Reg^t. went over upon Goat Island.^{1} to take thier Quarters theere, Joseph Congdon^2 a Deserter was brought into the Garrison last Evening and was Sent to the main Guard this Morning, he was taken up near Newlondon, the Day Continued Cold, I and Col Greene went over to Goat Island and Returned by Evening

4th. Nothing Remarkable happend this Day ——

November 5th, 6th, 1779. This morning we Rec^d orders for all the Continental

---

^{1} Goat Island is in Newport harbor; the Naval Torpedo Station is located on the island.

^{2} Joseph Congdon, of Lieut.-Col. Jeremiah Olney's Company. His name appears in the roll of Capt. Stephen Olney's Company, at Yorktown, as having participated in that engagement.

Troops to March to the westward, but the wind blew So hard that we Could not Cross the bay, in the afternoon, I Set off for home. got to bristol ferry[1] and the wind blu So hard that I Could not Cross, went to Mr Durfeys there Staid the night, in the morning Crost went to Warren breakfasted, then went to Providence there Dind then went to my own hous found all well

Novr. 7th. Still and Plesant Morning Nothing Remarkable happend this Day I tarried at home

Novr. — 8th — 1779. this Morning after breakfast I Set off for Camp. arrivd in Greenwich by twelve °Clock Dind with Genl. Stark, then went to the Reg^t. which lay about one Mile and half from Greenwich westward found all well,

9th. This morning Rec^d. Orders for Col Livingstons Reg^t. Col Webbs and Col Jacksons. to march the Next morning at Sunrise. My Reg^t. Col°. Greens and Col. Sherburnes the day after at Sunrise, this Day we were all a making out our Returns for Cloathing blankets &c.

Novr. 10th, 1779. This morning Col° Webbs Reg^t. marched off, Col°. Levingstons

---

[1] At the northern end of the island of Rhode Island.

Did not march till the afternoon Col Jacksons marched the Day before from providence this Night we Spent till two °Clock next morning delivering out Clothing to the Officers

Novr. 11th —, 1779. This Morning was Exceeding Cold we finished Delivering out the Cloathing to the Soldiers by Eleven °Clock. and Marched off the Ground. by twelve I tarried untill all the waggons were got under way then Gave the Charge of the Reg^t. to the Major, and went to Greenwich Dind with Col Greene, then went to See my familey, the Major returnd yesterday from Visiting his familey, and Col Olney wen^t for providence. for nine or ten Days

12th November, 1779. This Morning Ensign Roggers [1] Come to my hous going in Search of benoni Bishop [2] and Robert Gilley [3] two Deserters, after breakfast Ensign Roggers Set off, and before Noon Returnd with the Above Said Deserters, and went on after the Reg^t. with them Carried them to Vollentown there Deliverd them up to the Reg^t. and returnd

13th Novr., 1779. this Day Ensign Rog-

---

[1] John Rogers, appointed Ensign by General Assembly of Rhode Island, June, 1780, commission to date from May 1, 1779.

[2] Benoni Bishop, of Major Thayer's Company.

[3] Robert Gilly, of Major Thayer's Company.

gers Returnd, and went on for Smithfield, I went to Scituate for to buy Some beef Returnd at Evening Serj^t Noah Chaffe Come to My hous this Day after Some Deserters, and went to providence, by water and a Young man Saw Samuel Grant [1] a Deserter from my Reg^t I Sent them imeadetly in Search after him and they took him brought him to my hous by one oClock the Next Morning. freelove water man and husband was at my hous her Sister and Sweetheart.

14th Novr., 1779. fine Weather and a great number of people Come to My hous this Day. Serj^t Chaffe Come to me for Orders as he was Directed by Maj^r Thayer, and I Sent Grant to providence to the Goal, he allso brought News that William Edmans,[2] a deserter was taken up and brought to the furnice in Scituate,[3] and Col Olney had Sent for him to Providence Goal.

15th November, 1779. This Morning Sent my Servant to providence to get Some Salt, and got help to kill my Beef, but the ladd returnd and got none, as they would not Sell aney without they Could have provisions

---

[1] Samuel Grant, of Col. Angell's Company.

[2] William Edmunds, of Col. William Humphrey's Company.

[3] Scituate Furnace, the site of the present village of Hope, on the Pawtuxet River, near the line between Coventry and Scituate.

for it. theire was a great number of people at
my hous this Day

Novr. 16. fine weather, I was to have
Sett off for the Army this morning but as I
Could not git no Salt yesterday, Sent by M^r
Luther this Day and was determind Not to
goe forward untill I Could get Some, he Returnd at night, and had not got a handfull, thus
being Disapointd Did not go forward

November 17th, 1779. Clowdy and
Snowed very fast this morning I Sent my boy
off for North kingstown to Peter Phillips Esqr.
to See if he Could purchase me Some Salt,
Nothing Remarkable happend this Day

Novr. 18th. My boy I Sent to Northkings
Town Returnd this forenoon with two bushel
of Salt, which my frind Peter Phillips Esqr let
me have. John Usher and Thomas Smith both
Come to my hous this Day.

Novr. 19th, 1779. Sevear Cold this
morning. I was to have Set off for Camp but
my Cloathes not being Ready concluded to
tarry until the Next day morning.

Novr. 20th. A fine plesant Day, but I
was So much unwell that it prevented my Setting off for the army So I spent the Day at
home

21st. This morning it raind very hard,

which Still prevented me from going forward, and I Spent the day with my familey

November 22nd, 1779. Clowdy and raind a little this morning but Soon broak away. and after breakfast I Set off on my journey to join the Army and went to Volentown [1] to m[r]. Dorrances there Dind. then went on as far as Scotland to M[r] Forbes Tavern who married the widow Flint there put up for that Night.

Novr. 23rd. Left my lodgings Early this morning wint through Windham to M[r] Hills there breakfasted then went to Bolten [2] there dind from thence went to Hartford then put up at one M[r] Lords a privat hous. Where Doctor Cornelius was Quarterd. attending on Some Sick which was left behind of Gen[l]. Starkes Brigade

24th Novr., 1779. After breakfast this morning I went on my Journey to farmingtown 10 miles. from thence to Southerington 7 miles there Dind. then went to Waterbury 14 miles there put up for the Night. at one M[r] judds

---

[1] The towns at which stops were made serve to indicate one of the lines followed by travellers through Connecticut in early times. From Voluntown, at the eastern end of Connecticut, the course was northwesterly until Hartford was reached, where the course changed to southwest, ending at Danbury, att he western end of Connecticut.

[2] Bolton, Conn.

Tavern, here I got intelligence of my Reg^t. being in danbury by a Capt. in Genl. Glovers Brigade. who was on his way home on furlough

25th November, 1779. Left my lodgings this Morning before Sunrise went to one Mr Melleries Tavern Seven miles on a New road towards Woodbury there Breakfasted, then went through Wood Bury South bury to new Town there Dind 21 Miles then went to Danbury where I found the Reg^t. Col. Olney and Major Thayer were Quartered in a Grand hous Occupid by the widow Wollsey of Long Island

26th. Clowdy and Snowed this Day, in the Afternoon Col Greene and Griffen Greene [1] Arrived in town from Rhodeisland, on their way to head Quarters, and I Set off with them in as bad a Snow Storm as Generaly Ever Comes Rode about 9 miles there put up at a Public hous in the State of Newyork

November 27th, 1779. it Cleard off in the night and we Left our lodgings Early this morning it was Exceeding bad riding on acct of the Snow, though not more then Ancle Deep

---

[1] Griffin Greene, son of Jabez, Jr., and Susannah, born Feb. 16, 1749; chosen Paymaster, August, 1777; Major of Kentish Guards, May, 1778. By order issued Aug. 11, 1778, " Griffen Green Esq. is to act as Aid D. Camp to Major Gen. Greene." (Col. Sherburne's Orderly Book in Newport Historical Society.)

as it raind part of the night which made bad traveling we arrivd at the River opposit west point about Day light Dawn. and Crost over to the point. where We found great Difficulty in gitting our horses out of the boat. and Climbing the rocks, to git on the plain at the foot of the Mountains which when we had Accomplished Enquired for the Adj^t. General. where we found maney of our frends, Supt with the Adj^t. Genl. then I went with Major Peters [1] lodgd with him and Major Nicholson [2] Col Greene tarried with the adj^t. General. Mr Griffen Greene went with Genl. Patterson, we rode this Day 12 or 15 miles and Could get nothing for our [horses]

November 28th, 1779. This Morning I got up by break of Day went to view the forts the first was fort putnam [3] on a high

---

[1] This may refer to Peters, Andrew (Mass.), Captain of Read's Massachusetts Regiment, May to December, 1775; Captain 13th Continental Infantry, 1st January to 31st December, 1776; Major 2d Massachusetts, 1st January, 1777; Lieutenant-Colonel 15th Massachusetts, 1st July, 1779; resigned 26th November, 1779. (Died 5th February, 1822.) (Heitman's "Officers of the Continental Army.")

[2] Nicholson, George Chadine (N.Y.), Major 1st Canadian (Livingston's) Regiment, 6th May, 1777; retired 1st January, 1781. (Heitman's "Officers of the Continental Army.")

[3] Fort Putnam was located at the top of Mount Independence, nearly five hundred feet above the river.

It was built of stone in 1778 to complete a system of works to

Mountain. which may be properly Called the
American Giberalter, the next I went to was
fort Arnold[1] in both these forts was bumb proof
Suficient to hold what men it would take to
man the lines there was a fort on Every Emmi-
nence Some Distance round. after breakfast We
waited on his Excellency. had an Invitation to
dine with him but gitting nothing for our horses
went on for New Winsor, over the Mountains
through the High lands. over the highest
mountain I ever was upon we was about two
hours Climbing up the mountain. Some part
of the way I was affraid my hors would fall
backwards in Climbing up, was obliged to Stop
at Every opportunity when the land would
Admit of it to git breath. we got to New

secure the river from the passage of the enemy's ships. It was
named after the commander of the post, Gen. Israel Putnam.

This fort had an armament, Sept. 5, 1780, consisting of five iron
eighteen-pounders, two iron twelve-pounders, three brass pieces of
small calibre, and four brass 5½-inch mortars. It had two bomb-
proofs. — *Lossing.*

[1] Fort Arnold was one of the outposts in the line of defences at
West Point. It was situated upon "a commanding eminence above
the road leading to Buttermilk Falls."

From "Remarks on Works at West Point, a copy to be trans-
mitted to his Excellency General Washington, Sept., 1780," written
by Benedict Arnold, it appears that "Fort Arnold is built of Dry
Fascines and wood, is in a ruinous condition incompleat and subject
to take fire from Shells or Carcasses" its armament consisted of "one
iron twenty-four pounder, six iron eighteen pounders, one iron
twelve pounder, three iron three pounders, one brass four pounder
and eleven brass mortars of various calibres." — *Lossing.*

Winsor a little after Sunset but Could git nothing for our Selves or horses to Eat. went
on for Newbourgh. Applyd to Quartermaster
Mitchel for forrige for our horses who furnished
us with a little, then Sent a boy to get lodgings
for us which he did at an Old Dutch mans hous
Col Green and I applyd to the Cloather Gen[1].
and finished our business with him which was to
git Cloathing for our Reg[t]. or an Order for it
then went to our lodgings

29th Novr., 1779. this Morning after
breakfast I got My horses Shodd Crost the
North River over to fishkill Went on for Danbury Col Greene and M[r] Griffin Greene went for
Springfield So we parted about Six miles from
fishkill but Still Could git nothing for our
horses. till riding ten or twelve miles. there
Dind and fed our horses then went to Col°
Luttentons Tavern among the Mountains 21
Miles from fishkill there put up for the Night
one of Col° Levingstons Officers Came to this
tavern in the Evening on his way home on furlough

Novr. 30th, 1779. Left my lodgings
this morning after breakfast went on for Danbury Arrived there by one o Clock found all
well, the Gen. had Sent an Officer to Stamford
and along the Sea Coast to See if there was an

English fleet in the Sound and if there was not, he had orders from his Excellency by me. to march on the Brigade to join the grand Army in the Jerseys

Decr. 1st, 1779. Fine Plesant weather and Nothing Remarkable this forenoon in the afternoon one of the Serj[ts]. Viz. Serj[t] Hight [1] brought a very handsom patch Gound to my Quarters which he had taken from one M[rs] Thomas a Soldiers wife in the Regiment. which She had Stolen from a woman [2] at Updikes Newtown in the State of Rhode Island.   I took the Gound in order to Send it to the owner. and ordered all the Drums and fifes to parade and Drum her out of the Reg[t]. with a paper pind to her back, with these words in Cappital letters, /A THIEF/ thus She went off with Musick —

December 2d, 1779. An Exceeding Stormey Day which Detained us this Day from marching

3rd. This Day we was Making preparation for marching the next morning when there

---

[1] Sergt. Jonathan Hoight, of Cap. Thomas Hughes' Company.

[2] Waity Brown, of Updike's Newtown (Wickford), as stated in a memorandum at end of this part of the diary. There was a Waite Reynolds, of North Kingstown, who married Benjamin Brown, also of North Kingstown, Oct. 17, 1771, who may have been the person referred to.

Come news that the bridg over Croton River was broak down which detaind us another Day

4th. This Day Major Thayer Set off for Providence State Rhode Island on busness And we Remaind at our present Quarters

December 5th, 1779. This morning the Brigade marched we had not marched far before it begun to Snow and was Exceeding Cold and tedious I marched my Reg^t. about 18 or 20 miles there got my Reg^t. all into houses and good Quarters for my Self. but my waggons did not get up by Seven miles

Decr. 6th & 7th. A fine Clear morning. but Very Cold. and the Snow about ancle Deep. I got the troops Under way by a little after Sunrise, marched as far as within half a mile of kings ferry there lodged in the woods that Night Next Morning Turnd out at Break of Day marched to the ferry Crost hudsons River marched on to Kakaat there got the troops into houses. I went on a head and took my Quarters at Col Sherrads this Day we took up Samuel Dyer a Deserter from my Reg^t. and was trid by a Court martial. ordered to be whipt one hundred lashes on his Naked back

December 8th, 1779. Marched this Morning by a little after Day light went to Soverens tavern in Ranomapough, there halted,

and drew Some flower then went to Pumpton [1]
there barracked the troops. after Marching 22
Miles

Decr. 9th. This Day we lay Still for
our waggons to Come up, Col Levingstons
Reg[t]. &c Col° Sherburnes marched by us and
went in frunt and took Quarters, Gen[l]. Stark
Got up with the troops to Day

December 10th, 1779. A Rainey Day
and we lay Still thier I went to Dine with Gen[l].
Stark our Baggage Come up to Day.

Decr. 11th. A Clear and Cold morning.
the brigade Lay Still this day waiting for the
baggage to Come up

Decr. 12th. A Snowy morning. we Rec[d].
Orders not to March this Day on account of
its Storming, there Came Two Deers by my
Quarters, and was pursd By the Soldiers but
they Could not Ketch them.

13th December, 1779. This morning
it Raind but broak away and was Clear about
Eleven oclock and the Brigade Marched for
Morristown my Reg[t]. went about 16 miles.
great part of the way over Shoe in mud and
Some places up to the mens knees in water we
marched very fast untill Some time in the
Evening before we got to the place of our Dis-

---

[1] Pompton, N.J.

tination I put up at Col° Courtlands [1] a Gentleman from Newyork and proprietor of Courtlands Mannor [2] —

Scituate, 22d Novr., 1779. This Day Settled and ballanced all Accounts between M[r] Nathaniel Lovel and Col Israel Angell up to this Day

Wittness our hand

NATHANIEL LOVELL

I ANGELL

Expences Greens - - - 0 – 10 – 0
Dorrances - - - - - 3 – 6 – 0
Forbes - - - - - - -

Weighty Brown of Updikes Newtown North Kingstown gound found by Serj[t]. Hight

---

[1] Philip Van Courtlandt was a Colonel in the American army, having been appointed in 1776.

He served at the battle of Stillwater, and against the Indians on the frontier in 1778. In 1779–80 he was a member of the court-martial which was convened for the trial of Arnold.

For gallantry and meritorious conduct at the battle of Yorktown, he was raised to the brevet rank of Brigadier-General.

He accompanied General Lafayette on his tour through the states in 1824. He died at the Manor House, Nov. 5, 1831, aged eighty-two.

[2] The Van Courtlandt Manor was erected in 1773, and was an elegant brick mansion. A cut of the Van Courtlandt house may be seen in Lossing's "Field Book of the Revolution," Vol. II., p. 623.

The house is yet standing, and occupies a site in the present Van Courtlandt Park in the northern edge of the city of New York.

It has recently been placed by the authorities in the care of one of the hereditary patriotic societies, and has been converted into a museum and repository of relics, to which purpose it was dedicated with public festivities.

PART FIVE.

THE events which transpired between Aug. 10, 1780, and Sept. 30, 1780, form the subject of the fifth part of the diary. It finds the army encamped in Northern New Jersey, and from whence it moved to West Point, in New York. Here the regiment was located at the time of the treason of Arnold, and the diary terminates with the events following this monstrous affair.

August 10th, 1780. Clear and hott, this morning, the Brigade was Inspected by Baron Stuben[1] my Reg^t. was the first for In-

---

[1] Frederick William Von Steuben, Major-General in the Revolutionary Army, " was one of the best educated and most experienced soldiers of Germany." He held the rank of Lieutenant in the Seven Years' War, and had also held a position on the staff of Frederick the Great.

He arrived in America on the first day of December, 1777, and immediately addressed letters to Washington and to Congress offering his services in the American cause.

His superior military training and knowledge of tactics was of the greatest value to the American army, and through his efforts the troops were brought to a high grade of discipline.

In August, 1779, Baron Steuben, then Inspector-General of the

spection, and the Baron was Exceedingly pleasd with the mens array being in the best Order. Nothing Remarkable.

11th. The Division Court Martial whereof I was President was ordered to Assemble in order to finish the trial of Lt Boss of the 4th Pennsylvania Reg^t. but Some of the Members did not attend by which Reason no business was Done, there has ben a firing from one of the Enemys Gunboats in North River at our Guards but no harm done. Two Battallions paraded for Manoevering one of which I Commanded

12th. Clowdy dark Morning. and abundance of Thunder. but little rain. Nothing remarkable this day. I was much unwell.

United States Army, arrived in Providence on an official tour to inspect the corps of General Gates.

He compiled for the use of the army a work on military tactics, which was in use by the army of the United States for many years. Copies of it are now rare, the edition being limited to three thousand copies.

The story of his life and service in the cause of the Colonies is told in " The Life of Frederick William Von Steuben, Major-General in the Revolutionary Army," by Friedrich Kapp, New York, 1859.

His services as briefly stated by Saffel in his " Records of the Revolutionary War " are as follows: " Joins the army at Valley Forge; made Inspector-General; commands at Monmouth, June 28, 1778; made Major-General; commands at Virginia and Yorktown in 1781; receives 16,000 acres of land in Oneida County, N.Y. Congress, per act June 4, 1790, grants him an annuity of $2,500 for life, to commence Jan. 1, 1790. Died at Steubenville, N.Y., Nov. 28, 1795."

August 13th, 1780. Extreem hott, I was Exceeding Sick in the afternoon took a puke. and by not attending to the Doctors Directions in taking it all at a time. when I was to have taken only a part. it had like to Carried me out of the Land of the living a large fatague party went to dobbs Ferry to fortifying. a Number of Cannon was fir'd at our people from a brigg and a Galley in North River

14th. As hot as ever. I am much weller than yesterday, though but in a poor State of health. Nothing Remarkable this day

15th. This was thought to be the Hottest Day Ever known. no Circumstances Relative to the Army worth Mentioning

16th. the Extreem heat Continues. I was officer of the Day, Nothing Remarkable

17th August, 1780. Heat Continues. Dind at Head Quarters this morning 4 °Clock the Brigg and Galley belonging to the Enemy up North River went down past dobbs ferry Six Cannon and Hoitzers was fired at them but what Dammage they received is not known,

18th. This Day I went down to See the Light infantry. and went as low as English Neighbour Hood about 12 miles from Camp. Returnd by Sunsett, the officers presented me with a request this morning that I might have a Court of Inquirey into my Conduct at Springfield, as a report was Spread very preju-ditious to my Character

19th. Much Cooler this day then it had ben I was Scarce able to Sett up one hour. being So much unwell

20th August, 1780. This morning Seemd like October and Continued Cool the day, Each wing of the army was ordered to parade togeather. as they had had two Seperate parades before, news from Congress this day that was disagreable they having reduced the Officers wages 50 percent, and to pay them in a new omition of paper Money.

August 21st. The report of the Officers wages being Reduced. provd a mistake. Dind at Gen[l]. Greenes. Nothing Remarkable

22d. Cool Morning Two Battalions Man-oeverd this morning one of which I Com-manded the Barron was present himself. Rec. orders this Afternoon to march to tomorrow morning Seven °Clock, went to prepairing Accordingly.

23d. the Revelle beat as usual the Gen[l]. at 5 °Clock when the tents were Struck. the Assembly at Six when they troops all paraded, the March at Seven when they all Moved

forward Marching by the right, towards English
Neighbour hood. after Marching about 3 Miles
the Right Wing took a road leading to
Slaughtinburgh,[1] the Left a road to tennec and
English Neighbourhood where the road that
the right wing marched in fell in with the
road that the left took, these roads met on a
Large Plain at a place Calld Liberty poll[2] in
the vicinity of English Neighbourhood, here
the Army Encamped. this was an exceeding
hott Day

24th. Clear and hott. All the waggon
of the Army was Collected this day and in the
Evening went down to bergin[3] to bring off all
the forrage The light Infantry all went down
in frunt, and Gen[l]. Clintons Brigade marched
to fort Lee[4] at burdetts ferry part of the Right

---

[1] Probably Schraalenburgh, N.J.

[2] The original Liberty Pole, set up in 1765 and from which the
place took its name, was located near the spot where the present
Liberty Pole, set up by the Daughters of the Revolution, is placed,
at the intersection of Palisade avenue with the road leading from
Fort Lee, at Englewood, N.J.

Here in the days of the Revolution was the Liberty Pole Tavern,
a famous place of resort for the patriots of the neighborhood. For
many years, down to the middle of the present century, this tavern
was the voting-place for the whole township of Hackensack. The
house was destroyed some twenty years ago. A carefully made
sketch of it, showing the original Liberty Pole, is in the possession
of Miss Elizabeth Sedgewick Vaill, of Demarest, N.J.

[3] Bergen, N.J.

[4] This fortification was situated upon a sort of plateau, about

wing marched all so, I went off with a number
of Gentlemen to fort Lee where I had a view
of the Enemy —

August 25, 1780. Exceeding hott, there
was a Considerable firing this day towards New
York but nothing remarkable Come to hand —

26th. Extreme Hott. the Regiment was
Mustered this Morning for the months of
June and July, the waggons that went a forrag-
ing begun to return this morning, and in the
afternoon I and Lt Jencks of my Regiment
went down to the Infantry Camp. to See Major
Thayer and the officers as I had Rec^d. a letter
from the State Inclosing an Act of the General
Assembly. offering the Officers and Soldiers of
the Continental Battalions Land for their De-
preciation but the troops had not Returnd.
So we rode to meet them which we did in bergin about Seven miles from their Camp, they
had just hanged a man for plundering the inhabitants. he was a Pensylvanian[1] one of Col

three hundred feet above the river, at the present landing and
village of Fcrt Lee, N.J.

A little above was a redoubt opposite Jefferys' Hook to cover
the *chevaux-de-frise* in the river. — *Lossing's "Field Book of the
Revolution."*

[1] Probably the soldier referred to by Thatcher under the same
date as being executed for robbery. " He was one of five who broke
into a house with their arms and robbed the inhabitants of a sum
of money and valuable articles." " He conducted," says Thatcher,
" with fortitude at the gallows."

Humptons Reg[t]. he was hanged by orders of the Commanding Officer without a trial, I Returnd back to my Quarters about Ten °Clock in the Evening.

August 27th, 1780. Violent hott and Dry — after breakfast went in Company with a number of the Gentlemen Officers across the woods to north River to a place Called Spiten Devils Creek against king bridg. from thence Down the river to burdeets ferry at fort Lee. we had a grand prospect of all the Enemys Incampments on York Island returnd to Camp before Eleven °Clock. there found Maj[r]. Thayer and Some of the officers of the Infantry.

28th August, 1780. Clear and hott I Set off into the Country this morning on business went to hackensack,[1] Acquackanack[2] and Springfield about 35 miles I Suffered greatly with the heat this day it being the driest time in this Country I ever See, lodged at M[r] Lanarcnus.

29th. Set of this morning for Newark, from thence to Hackensack, in Newark fell in Company with Cap[t]. Higgens[3] who was a

---

[1] Hackensack, N.J.   [2] Aquakinunk, N.J.

[3] Heitman mentions a " Higgins, Robert (Va.), 1st Lieutenant 8th Virginia, 12th March, 1776; Captain, 1st March, 1777; was a prisoner in September, 1778; transferred to 2d Virginia, 12th February, 1781, and served to . . . ", who may have been the officer referred to.

prisoner out on Parole, he was agoing to head Quarters and rode in Company with me to hackensack. where I was taken So Ill that I Could go no further where we halted and Staid at a Dutchmans

30th August, 1780. Left our lodgings Early this Morning went to Camp and Breakfasted, found all well.

31st. Cooler then it had ben, and look^t like for rain, there was a heavy firing of Cannon towards the hook, which Continued all the day, and at Night there was a heavey thunder Shower with Extreem hard thunder and Sharp lightening, which was the first Shower that had ben in a longe time here and the Earth was the most perched that I Ever Saw it in any part of the world that I was in, I Saw tobaco here that was killd with the Drouth —

September 1st, 1780. Cool and pleasant this Morning. I was exceeding much not well. The firing of Cannon Still Continued at the hook the Same as yesterday but Nothing Remarkable this day,

Septr 2nd, 1780. Clowdy and Cold with the wind in the Northeast and had raind a Considerable in the Night, Continued raining the Day, in the afternoon Rec^d Orders for the Army to march tomorrow morning 5 °Clock,

this order was Countermanded and the Army
was to march at Eight oClock Instead of 5,

September 3rd, 1780. An Exceeding
Rainey Morning, which Prevented the Army
from marching Agreable to the Orders of yesterday. L^t. Col^o Olney was the Officer of the
day yesterday, and got lost in going the rounds
Last night. lay in the woods till day Light.
Cleard off this Afternoon plesant. Orders Came
again for us to march tomorrow morning

September 4th. Clear and Cooler then
it had ben for Some time past, the Army got
under way by ten °Clock, but met with Some
Obstructions by Bridges breaking, which detaind the rear till Eleven when the whole moved
off the ground, we marched by the right, Crost
what is called New bridg.[1] over hackensack
River, turnd to the right up the River towards
Toppan and Encamped. on a high Ridge of
land in a place Calld Stenrappie [2]

September 5th, 1780. A Gold morning. I Still Remaind unwell Nothing Remarkable happend this Day till Evening when
there Came News that all our Army to the

---

[1] At the time of the Revolution this was called "the New
Bridge." The locality is now New Bridge, N.J.

[2] Steenraupie, a local name signifying Stony Arabia, reaching
along the ridge near Oradell and towards Kinderkamack, N.J.
(*E. K. Bind, in New York " Evening Post."*)

Southward was killd taken and Disperst, Gen[1]
Gates who Commanded had by Some means
made his Escape,[1]

And rode 180 Miles in three Days before he
Stopt, and then Could not tell what had become
of his Army, but had Sent back a flagg to Enquire after them   Thus Eands the Day with
Bad news

September 6th, 1780. Cool weather
for the Season, Nothing Remarkable this Day,
my Illness was more Sevear then Yesterday.

7th. Co°l. I was freer from pain this
morning then I had ben for Several days past.
Nothing Remarkable happend this Day, Except Gen[1]. Sullivan arrived in Camp on his way
to Congress being a member of that body —

8th. Clear and Plesant. I was Officer of
the day but Could not attend to the Duty being
So much Unwell,

September 9th, 1780. Clear and Very
Cool. Rec[d] News this morning of the Death
of the Honourable Brigadier General Poor.[2] who

---

[1] This refers to the disastrous battle of Camden, N.C., and the
ignominious flight of Gates, who, says Fiske, "caught in the
throng of fugitives at the beginning of the action, was borne in
headlong flight as far as Clermont, where, taking a fresh horse, he
made the distance of nearly two hundred miles to Hillsborough in
less than four days."

[2] Brig.-Gen. Enoch Poor was a native of New Hampshire.
He was a Colonel in the Continental army in the expedition against

departed this life Last Evening after a Short
Illness of the putred feavour, the News from
the Southward. Came more favourable this
day then it had ben it is Said there is a letter
from the Governor of Virginia that the Marry-
land Troops[1] With one regiment from North

Canada in 1776, where he served with distinction. He was afterwards at Crown Point and was one of the twenty-one inferior officers who signed a remonstrance against the decision of a council
of officers there, consisting of Generals Gates, Schuyler, Sullivan,
Arnold, and Woedtke, when it was resolved that the post was unten-
able and that the army retire to Mount Independence.

He was appointed Brigadier in 1777 and served in that capacity
in the battles in which Burgoyne was defeated and captured. He
soon afterwards joined the army under Washington in Pennsylvania. He was in the camp at Valley Forge, and with his brigade
was among the first troops that commenced a pursuit of the British
across New Jersey in the summer of 1778.

He fought gallantly in the battle of Monmouth which succeeded.
He commanded a brigade of light infantry in 1780, in which service
he died, near Hackensack, in New Jersey.

His funeral was attended by Washington and Lafayette and a
long line of subordinate officers and soldiers. On account of the
vicinity of the enemy the usual discharges of cannon were omitted.
Rev. Israel Evans, Chaplain to the New Hampshire brigade, delivered a funeral discourse.

General Poor was buried in the churchyard at Hackensack,
where a humble stone, with the following inscription, marks his
grave: " In memory of the Hon. Brigadier-General Enoch Poor, of
the State of New Hampshire, who departed this life on the 8th day
of September, 1780, aged 44 years."

General Poor was greatly esteemed by Lafayette, who, it is said,
was much affected on visiting his grave when in this country in
1825. — *Notes in Lossing's " Field Book of the Revolution," Vol. II.,
pp. 122-123.*

[1] Of the gallantry displayed by the Second Maryland Brigade,
under command of General Gist, at the battle of Camden, Fiske in

Carolina Stood their ground fought with Chargd Bayonetts 15 minuts. that they Cutt the brittish hors nearly all off. the los on our Side was between 3 and 400 Men.

10th Septr. 1780. Raind a little this Morning. but Soon Cleard off. and was hot I went down to the Infantry, from thence to Gen[l]. Greenes to talk with him upon the unhappy affair of mine. he advised me Call a Court of Enquirey imeadetly. Returned to Camp. in the afternoon the Remains of Gen[l] Poore was Intered at hackensack Church yard. admidst a Numerous Concours of People [1]

---

his "American Revolution" says : "The Second Maryland Brigade, . . . after twice repelling the assault of Lord Rawdon, broke through his left with a splendid bayonet charge and remained victorious upon that part of the field until the rest of the fight was ended; when being attacked in flank by Webster (the right division consisting of a small corps of light infantry and the 23d and 33d Regiment), these stalwart troops retreated westerly by a narrow road between swamp and hillside and made their escape in good order."

[1] Thatcher in his Military Journal describes more minutely this military funeral and procession : "A regiment of light infantry in uniform, with arms reversed; four field pieces; Major Lee's Regiment of light horse; General Hand and his brigade, the major on horseback; two chaplains : the horse of the deceased, with his boots and spurs suspended from the saddle, led by a servant; the corpse, borne by four sergeants and the pall supported by six general officers. The coffin was of mahogany, and a pair of pistols and two swords, crossing each other and tied with black crape, were placed on top. The corpse was followed by the officers of the New Hampshire Brigade, the officers of the brigade of light infantry, which the deceased had lately commanded. Other officers fell in promis-

Septr. 11th, 1780. This day I applyd to the Commander In Chief for a Court of Enquiry which he was pleasd to order Nothing Remarkable this Day

Septr. 12th. A Soldier [1] in Col° Stewarts

cuously, and were followed by His Excellency General Washington and other general officers. Having arrived at the burying yard, the troops opened to the right and left, resting on their arms reversed, and the procession passed to the grave, where a short eulogy was delivered by the Rev. Mr. Evans. A band of music with a number of drums and fifes played a funeral dirge, the drums were muffled with black crape, and the officers in the procession wore crape round the left arm. The regiment of light infantry were in handsome uniform and wore in their caps long feathers of black and red. The elegant regiment of horse commanded by General Lee, being in complete uniform and well disciplined, exhibited a martial and noble appearance. No scene can exceed in grandeur and solemnity a military funeral. The weapons of war reversed and embellished with the badge of mourning, the slow and regular step of the procession, the mournful sounds of the muffled drum and deep-toned instruments, playing the melancholy dirge, the majestic and solemn march of the war horse, all combine to impress the mind with emotions which no language can describe and which nothing but the reality can paint to the liveliest imagination. General Poor was from the State of New Hampshire. He was a true patriot, who took an early part in the cause of his country, and during his military career was respected for his talents and his bravery, and beloved for the amiable qualities of his heart. But it is sufficient eulogy to say that he enjoyed the confidence and esteem of Washington."

[1] " HEADQUARTERS STEENRAPIE Sept. 12th. 1780.

"David Hall, a soldier in Col. Steward's Battalion of Light Infantry, convicted, at a Genl Court Martial, whereof Col. Courtland is President, of plundering an inhabitant of money and plate, and being condemned to death, is to be executed at half past 4 o'clock this afternoon —

" Fifty men properly officered frome very Brigade in the Army,

Battalion was hanged this day on the Grand
Parade for Plundering the Inhabitants agreable
to the Sentence of a Gen¹ Court Martial : the
Order for my Court of Enquirey was in
Orders. a Number of Savages of the Onido
Nation Came to head Quarters this Day.
there was the hardest thunder this Evening I
ever knew)

Septr. 13th, 1780. The whole Army
was Ordered yesterday in After orders. to
parade on their Brigade Parades at open Order
to make as Great a Show as possible, to be reviewed by the Commander in Chief, and the
Indian Chiefs of the Onido Nation, the Brigadᵉ
of Gen¹ Starks was Reviewed about 9 in the
Morning with a Ratinue of all the Gen¹. Officers of the Army and Great part of the field
Officers and all the Savages of note, after which

---

to attend in the rear of Genl. Patterson's Brigade : — It has been
much the Gen'ls desire to prevent enormities of this kind which
are as repugnant to the principles of the cause in which we are
engaged as oppressive to the inhabitants and subversive of that order
and discipline which must characterize every well regulated Army.

"The Gen'l again exhorts officers and soldiers of every rank to
pay the closest attention to the conduct of their men and to use
every precaution to prevent the soldiers from rambling and com-
mitting such outrages, the subject of daily complaint and represen-
tation to him. It is highly incumbent on them to do this, to prevent the consequences which will follow as he is determined to
show no favor to soldiers who are convicted of these pernicious
and disgraceful offences." — *Rev. Order of Gen. Washington, p. 102.*

we attended at the Court. but one member not Comming no business Could be Done. It was a very Rany afternoon but Nothing Remarkable happened

September 14th, 1780. Clear and Cool this Morning the Court of Enquiry Met and proceeded to Enquire into my Conduct on the 23rd of June and Examined all Evidences against me and adjurned til the next day 9 °Clock Nothing Remarkable.

Septr. 15th, 1780. Clear and Cold. I attended the Court this morning, but Major Reid one of the members was through mistake Sent on Command and no business Could be done. I applyd to the Adjutant Genl. to git him Releaved. which he promist me Should be done the next day we got news this day that the french fleet was on the Coast. Nothing more remarkable

September 16th, 1780. A fine Plesant day the Court not meeting I went down to the Infantry. we had news that Admiral Rodney was Come to the hook. and that the french fleet was in his rear it was reported that there is 13 Sail of the Line English and 25 french this I think is news enough for this day

17th Septr. Plesant weather. the Court of Enquiry out this day and finished the Business,

His Excellency Set off it is Said for hartford [1]
this Morning maney repoarts Concerning the
french fleet but Nothing to be depended upon
wrote to the Governor

18th Septr. Fine weather, and Nothing
Remarkable this day, till the Orders of the
day Come out, when the proceedings of the
Court of Enquiry Come to light in the following words. At a Court of Enquiry Calld
by desire of Col Angel to Enquire into a Report Relative to his being absent from his
Regiment in the Action at Springfield the 23rd
of June last. Col° Nixon President   The Court
having heard and duly Considered the Evidences, are unanimously of Opinion that Col
Angell was in the Action at Springfield on the
23rd of June last with his Regiment. and in the
Execution of his duty, and Behaved like a
Brave and Good officer [2] — Thus Ends the day

---

[1] Under date of the 20th Thatcher notes, " His Excellency General Washington, with the Marquis de la Fayette and General Knox,
with a splendid retinue, left the camp on the 17th instant, bound to
Hartford in Connecticut, to have an interview with commanding
officers of the French fleet and army which have lately arrived at
Rhode Island." The army, during the absence of General Washington, was under command of Gen. Nathanael Greene, of Rhode
Island.

[2] Under the date June 29, 1780, from his headquarters at Rama-
paugh, General Washington wrote to Governor Greene of Rhode
Island, " The gallant behavior of Coll. Angells' regiment on the
23rd inst, at Springfield, reflects the highest honor upon the officers

September 19th, 1780. A Raney wett morning, by an After order which Came to hand last Evening the army was to hold themselves in Readiness to march at a moments warning, it Clard off before noon or left raining Steadily, but was Showery till near night. I was Appointed a member to Settle a dispute [1] between Baron Stuben, and Col hazen, [2] the

---

and men. They disputed an important pass with so obstinate a bravery, that they lost upwards of forty in killed, wounded and missing, before they gave up their ground to a vast superiority of force." — *R.I. Col. Records, Vol. IX., p. 151.*

An account of the battle of Springfield, written by Wm. Maxwell to His Excellency Governor Livingston from " Jersey Camp near Springfield *14th June,* 1780," may be found in "Historical Magazine," 1859, Vol. III., p. 211.

[1] This dispute probably grew out of the affair for which Colonel Hazen was tried by court martial Sept. 17, 1780.

It appears from the Revolutionary Orders of General Washington No. 73, Colonel Hazen was tried for " Disobedience of orders and unmilitary conduct on the march from Tappan to the Liberty Pole," in halting the brigade under his command without any orders from the general commanding the division; this produced a " vacancy in the left column of near half a mile; " he was also accused of falsely asserting he had received orders from General Stark ordering him to do so.

Colonel Hazen was acquitted of the charges, and the finding of the court martial was approved by General Washington, and Colonel Hazen was released from arrest. No special mention is found of a controversy between the colonel and Steuben in the Orders of the Commander-in-chief. — *See Rev. Order of Gen. Washington, p. 105.*

[2] Moses Hazen was appointed Colonel of the Second Canadian Regiment in 1775. He commanded at Montreal for a short time. Afterwards he was appointed Colonel of a regiment called Con-

disput was Left to the 7 oldest Officers Commanding the 7 lines from the 7 States here in Service Newhampsheer, Col Cilley, Massachusetts Genl. Glover, Rhodeisland Col Angell. Connecticutt Gen¹. Persons New York Genl Clinton, New Jersy Col Dayton, Pennsylvania Gen¹. St Clair. a troublesom world this. as Soon as one gits out of trouble them Selves, are Calld upon to Settle Disturbances with others all the Gentlemen met but did no business, and Adjurnd till the 21ˢᵗ. as the whole Army was ordered to march to-morrow morning, to be under way by ten °Clock at furthest,

September 20th, 1780. A Clowdy morning, the General was beat this morning at Seven oClock, the baggage fild off at Eight, the Assembly beat at 9 the troops marched a little past ten went to Tappan and Encamped upon the Same Ground we went from the 23ʳᵈ of August past. it Raind Some this Day, and Remaind Clowdy the whole Day.

---

gress's Own. He was in the battles of Germantown and Brandywine.

Having charge of prisoners in Pennsylvania, he was ordered to designate, by lot, a British officer for retaliation in the case of Huddy (which may be found treated at length in Lossing's " Field Book," 2-160).

He died at Troy, New York, Jan. 30, 1802, aged sixty-nine years. — *Lossing's " Field Book of the Revolution," Vol. II., p. 174.*

Heitman gives the date of his death as Feb. 3, 1803.

Septr. 21st. a Rany morning but Soon broak away the Gentlemen met again this day to Settle the dispute between Barron Stuben and Col Hazen, but did not finish the business, went to dobbs ferry in the afternoon on our way back a merry Scean happened Gen¹ Stark goining to water his hors at a place Call'd the Stole, mired him, and got him into the mud and mire. the Gen¹. Got out without aney damage Except bedaubing himself with mud, the adj. Gen¹. allso mired his hors. but he got out without difficulty. Gen¹. Stark was drawd out by the Soldiers

Septr. 22nd, 1780. Foggy, but Soon broak away hot. the Gentlemen met this day at Gen¹ Sᵗ Clears and Setteled the dispute between Major Gen¹. Barron Stuben and Col Hazen, to the Satisfaction of both parties there was a heavey Cannonade this morning Supposd at kings ferry but Soon heard it was at tallows point a little below, a british fregit lying there Gen¹. Arnold ordered two heavey peaces down with one or two hoitzers in the night and opend his Batterey on her this morning when She was obligd to tow of, after having near 100 Shot at her.

Septr. 23d, 1780. A foggy morning but Soon Cleard off hott. Nothing Remarkable

the french Minister [1] Came into Camp yesterday morning and Sett off this morning for
Rhode Island

September 24th, ——. a Clowdy, but
Soon Cleard away hot and Remaind Exceeding
hot for the Season of the year till the afternoon
when it began to thunder and was a Considerable
of thunder and lightening, and rain The Enemy
landed from their Ship and Sloop in North
River this morning, a little below haverstraw
and bunt Maj^r. Smiths hous and all the Grain
and hay he had he had his barn hay and Grain
burnt last year by the brittish privats I Capt
Tew and Hews Rode up along Side of North
River 6 or 7 Miles. then turnd over the Mountain in a Valle or low place & Came into the
Road leading from Charles Town to Toppan,
Arrived in Camp before Sunset just as it began
to rain hard.

---

[1] Anne Cæsar de la Luzerne was born in Paris in 1741. He
first entered the army and was engaged in the Seven Years' War,
during which he obtained the rank of Colonel. He afterwards
turned his attention to diplomacy and became distinguished as an
ambassador to various courts of Europe. His official relations with
the United States Government were of four years' duration, and by
his friendly services he gained the strong approbation of Congress
and the warm regard of Washington. In 1781 Harvard University
conferred upon him the degree of LL.D. In 1783 he returned to
France and was sent ambassador to London, where he died Sept.
14, 1791. He came to this country in the same ship with John
Adams, then the American Minister. — *Stone.*

September 25th, 1780. Rec^d. Orders yesterday. or last Evening for all the whole Army to be under Arms this day at ten °Clock A.M. and formd in line of battle on a Ridg of high land west of orrang Town, then Changed their frunt to the right, this Manoever was performd by Signals, the first Cannon was a Signal for the troops to assemble on their Brigade parades, the 2nd Gun for them to march off, and form the line, 3rd Gun for them to Change their frunt to the right 4th gun for the Brigades to march off to their Camps. all this was performd with great precision, the troops was dismist by three °Clock — we had a Cool day for our Manoevering there being So much thunder yesterday and Last Evening

September 26th, 1780. The most Extraordinary affair happened yesterday that Ever has taken place Since the war, General Benedict Arnold who Commanded at west point went to the enemy,[1] His Excellency the Commander in Chief having ben to Hartford to meet the

---

[1] Arnold's treason is too well understood to need any account of it here. It certainly is invested with a peculiar vividness and new interest by reading these lines written by a man of such high patriotic impulses as the writer who was at hand when this most horrible episode of the Revolution took place. For an account of a "Procession in Honour of Arnold?" through the streets of the city of Philadelphia, Sept. 30, 1780, see "The Historical Magazine," 1861, Vol. V., p. 276.

French Gen¹. and Admiral, was on his way to join the army and yesterday the Adjᵗ. General ¹ of the Brittish Army was taken at Tarry Town as a Spye by three Militia men ² the news Soon reached west point, and on the Appearence of His Excellencey Comming to the post, Gen¹ Arnold went down to the River Side with Six men with him got into a boat went down the river to the English Friggat ³ that Lay there and went on board of her, and She Imeadetly Set Sail for New York, and by the best information he had ben Carrying on a treacherous Corrispondence with the Enemy. and had agreed to Sell them that post with all the men, but Heavens directed it otherways. on Receiving this intelligence, the whole Army was ordered to be ready to march as Soon as possible, we

---

¹ Maj. John André, Adjutant-General of the British army. An interesting account of Major André by Colonel Tallmadge is in "Historical Magazine," 1859, Vol. III., p. 229.

² John Paulding, David Williams, and Isaac Van Wert. Congress subsequently directed that each of these receive annually two hundred dollars in specie, or its equivalent, during their life; a silver medal was also awarded each, " one side of which shall be a shield with this inscription : *Fidelity*, and on the other the following motto : *Vincit amor Patriæ.*" These Washington was directed to present to them with a copy of the resolution of Congress. A letter reflecting on the patriotism and integrity of the captors of André, written by Gen. Joshua King, a Lieutenant in Colonel Sheldon's Regiment of Light Dragoons, and who first had charge of André, is printed in " The Historical Magazine," 1857, Vol. I., p. 293; see also pp. 313-375.

³ British sloop-of-war " Vulture."

all turnd out went to Cooking and packing up their Baggage the pennsylvania line marched of and left their Baggage to follow it being Expected that the Enemy would attempt to take west point this night the News Come to us alittle after midnight, had not this horrid Treason ben discovered America would have Rec^d. a deadly wound if not a fatal Stabb.

Septr. 27th, 1780. Clowdy and Cold with a high wind from the Northeast, begun to Storm about the middle of the day, and was a Cold rany Afternoon, we had News Come this day that on Joseph Smith [1] was taken up as a Spye from the Enemy and brought to west point where the Commander in Chief was, he Came out of New York with M^r. Andrew the Brittish adjutant General and it was thought that they would both Grace a halter togeather.

Septr. 28th, 1780. It Cleard away this Morning and was cold, after dinner I with a Number of the Officers of the Army road out to Meet His Excellencey on his return to the Army, but after riding Six or Seven miles heard

---

[1] This was Joshua Smith, a confederate of André's. He was tried by court martial, but there being no positive proof against him, he escaped death, but was ordered into confinement, but after several months, either from lack of vigilance on the part of his keepers or from indifference, he was allowed to escape to New York. — *Thatcher.*

he had taken another road, therefore turnd
another way back without Seeing him, M^r
Smith and the Brittish Adj^t. Genl. was allso
Comming on with a Guard of draggoon

Septr. 29th. The two prisoners Come to
Camp last evening, a flagg Came this day from
the Enemy Sir Hary Clinton made a demand
of Mr Andrew the Kings adj^t Genl, Saying he
Came out as a flagg and ought not to be detaind.

Septr. 30th, 1780. A board of Genl.
Officers Sat this day on Mr Andrew and con-
demnd him as a Spy, to Suffer death, the Commander in Chief approvd the Sentence and
ordered it put in Execution tomorrow five
oClock in the afternoon, a flagg was Sent from
head Quarters by the way of Elizabethtown to
the Enemy. and one Came from the Enemy to
dobbes ferry, and brought a number of things
from the Enemy to Maj^r Andrews his Servant
Came in the flagg.   I was Officer of the Day.

PART SIXTH.

THE concluding part of the diary begins with Feb. 14, 1781, and ends April 3, 1781. It details the last days of Colonel Angell's services in the army, of his journey from his home in Johnston, R.I., to West Point and return, and also includes a few days of retirement, after long years of faithful and conspicuous service with the Rhode Island Continental line.

Feby. 14th, 1781. Left my hous this Morning went to Mr Dorrances [1] in Voluntown 16 Miles then breakfasted went to Mr Reppley in Scotland 16 Miles then Dined then went to M^r. Hill in Lebanon 10 Miles there put up for the day 42

Feby. 15th, 1781. Left my lodgings early this morning went to Mr white Breakfasted then went to Hartford but could get no

---

[1] Dorrance's Tavern was a popular place of resort. It was not unlike most of the public houses at this period, and it is related that fast young men of most respectable families " drank Geneva rum on a wager at Dorrance's Tavern till all were drunk," and then started off " for a Voluntown frolic." — *Larned,* " *Windham County,*" *Vol. II., p. 235.*

ainner then rode about three miles on towards Farmington there Din'd then went to Farmington there tarried — 42 miles

Feby. 16th, 1781. Left my Lodgings this Morning went on about Six miles then Breakfasted and got one of my horses shod then went to Waterbury there Din'd then went to South Bury Doctor Grahams then put up for the Night I met a Number of the men of my Regt a going home this Day.

Feby. 17th, 1780 (?). Left my Lodgings this morning went on to Newtown from thence to Danbury there Din'd then went on for Camp but missing my way and being benighted put up at a log hous tavern in the mountains where for fear of being Rob'd could sleep but little.

Feby. 14th, 1781.

Paid at Dorrances Tavern	£o –	4 –	o
do at Rippleys in Scotland	o –	3 –	10
Paid for Oats	o –	1 –	o
Paid Mr Hills	o –	6 –	o
do at Mr White	o –	4 –	5
Do for Oats	o –	1 –	o
Do for ferriage	o –	1 –	o
Do		3 –	6
Do for lodgings	o –	8 –	4
Do for Oats and Breakfast	o –	3 –	o

Do for Dinner and hors Baiting	4 - 6	
Do Lodgings Suppers hors Keep- ing Doctor Grahams	0 - 9 - 4	
Do Breakfast	0 - 3 - 2	
Do Dinner	0 - 5 - 10	
carried over	2 - 18 - 11	
Supper and lodging		
Hors keeping &c	0 - 9 - 0	
Breakfast	0 - 2 - 6	
Sum brought over	2 - 18 - 11	

Total Expenses to Camp   3 - 1 - 15

To my Expences from Camp to West Point and back from the 21st of Feb to the 22   £0 , 9 , 0

To my Expences in paying of the men and going to west point from the 24th to the 27   0 - 12 - 0

March 10-1781 To my Expences from West Point to New Winsor   0 - 7 - 0

To my Expenses while at West Point paid Mr Mandaill   1 - 7 - 0

To Cash paid Rufus¹ for the Expences of get'ing the horses to Camp   0 - 10 - 0

6 - 6 - 4

¹ Rufus Chapman.

16 March To Cash paid Rufus   £0 – 9 – 0

18 To Cash for my Expences } 0 – 6 – 0
    while at West Point

19 To Cash paid the widow
    Brewer   2 – 11 – 9

20 To Cash paid   0 – 8 – 0

21 To Cash paid for myself and } 0 – 9 – 0
    hors keeping

Do To Cash for Oats   0 – 1 – 6

Do To Cash fŏr Dinner and
    baitings for Horses   0 – 5 – 1

To Cash paid Coles Tavern }
    for his hors keeping and } 0 – 10 – 6
    lodging

for hors hire   0 – 4 – 6

for hors keeping   0 – 6 – 0

For hors keeping and lodging   0 – 11 – 0

For hors keeping and breakfast   0 – 8 – 0

To Dinner and baiting   0 – 3 – [ ]

To hors hire in getting the
    Waggon along   0 – 5 – [ ]

               ——————
               6 – 18 – 10

24 March 1781.

Paid for hors Keeping and
    lodging   £0 – 16 – 6

To Cash for baiting	0	1	6
To Cash for do		1	2
25 To Cash for Entertainmt		11	6
To Cash for Dinner an baiting		8	6
Brought over from the other Pages	13	5	3
To Cash for hors hire	0	4	6
To Cash paid Peleg Peck for hors hire	0	3	0
To Cash paid Elesha Barns for hors hire	0	2	6
To Cash paid Crage for hors keeping	0	9	0
To Mony paid Rufus for Expences	1	4	0
	17	7	5

My Baggage was twelve days in Comming from West Point

Feby. 18th, 1781. Left my lodging this morning went to Camp found all well the men was so Rejoist at seeing me that they gave three Chears I immeditly went to paying off the troops

19th. Continued Close to my hutt paying the men Col° Greene Sent me a billet desiring me to Come to his Quarters this Evening but

I could not attend on account of paying the men off.

20th. This day I finished paying all Except the light Infantry which marched off the day I come into Camp the Regt. had orders to march tomorrow for west point.

21st. The troops marched this Morning agreeable to the Orders of yesterday I set off with them went to Colo Greene Quarters there Din'd then went to west Point Crost the River but could not get my hors over Returned after Dark Recrost a Miry Marsh to a hous where we got lodgings but nothing for ourselves or horses to Eat.

22d. This morning it Storming I and Col. Greene sett off to go the Point or Fort but met the Greatest part of the troops a Returning Againe having lain on Constitution Island [1] all the night in the Storm as they Got but one boat load over after I and Col° Greene Crosst before the boats was carried away by the Ice with five men in it the Men nor boat Could not be heard of this day. by Eleven o'clock

---

[1] Constitution Island lies opposite West Point; a substantial work called Fort Constitution was located on the island. One end of the immense chain which was stretched across the Hudson, May, 1778, to prevent the passage of the enemy's ships, was anchored on this island just below the present steamboat landing. Links of this chain may yet be seen at West Point.

Col. Green and myself went to his Q^{rs} from thence I went to the hutts found Capt Brown preparing for to Defend the baggage by making a block house of one of the huts

23d Feby. A Stormy Day I remaind this Day in the hutts.

24th. This Day went to Col° Greens Qrs there tarried all Night the Troops that marched for the point the 21 and Came back to the New Hampshire hutts Marched again to Day.

25th. Col. Greene and myself Sett of for the point Early in the Morning went to Mr Mandavils there left our horses then went to Cross the ferry but found it all Blockt up with the Ice we then Crost the flatts upon the Ice to Constitution Island where we Crost just before Night on our way Cros the Ice Ensign John Rogers fell through over a deep Creek ketched and hung by his arms we Indeavored to get rails to throw to him but could find none but some short peaces at length I thought of tying my Great Coat and Col Greenes together and then tying them to a Stick with the help of two little boys got it to him & Drawed him out but I would not have run the risk I did for all the State of New York had it not been to save life   Storm'd near all this Day.

26th Feby. We Spent this day in trying

to Cross the ferry which we Effected just at Sunsett tarried at Mr Mandavils

27th Feby, 1781. Left Mr Mandavils this morning after Breakfast went to Col. Lawrences Q^rs Peeks kill there met Lt Joseph Wheaton and paid the money for the Infantry to him then went to the hutts and there dined lodged at the Widow Brewers.

28th Feby. This day was plesant as Summer I spent the Same at the hutts at night went to the Widow Brewer there tarried.

March 1st, 1781. After Breakfast went to Col° Greenes Quarters there Spent the Day it being Clowdy and Cold and allso tarried this night with Col° Greene in the Evening there came a letter from Genl Heath Informing Col. Greene that the French Ships that went from New-Port had taken the Romolus of fifty guns and Nine sail of privateers and transports of Chesepeck Bay.

March 2d, 1781. Clowdy weet and Cold after Breakfast Col. Greene and I went to the hutts the man I had Sent after my horses return'd this day without them the Order being from Col. Greene and not from the D. Q. M General was Obligid to Send off again Din'd at the hutts then went to the Widow Brewers where I proposed to stay Col. Greene went to his Quarters

March 3d, 1781. Good weather and Nothing Remarkable Spent the Day at the hutts tarried at the widow Brewers

4th. Clear and plesant the Baggage of the Reg^t that was left at the hutts was ordered on for west Point as was all the troops Except a Guard of 42 men I sent Rufus Chapman [1] after horses

5th. Clowdy before breakfast Rufus return'd from fishkill and had got no horses upon which I set off Imeadetly for west point It soon began to Storm and stormed very hard I arrived at Mr Mandavels by 12 oclock where I put up for this day and night Col Green Come from the point in the evening.

March 6th, 1781. This morning after breakfast I & Col Greene went over to the Point he being president of a Court Martial after dining on the point Returned to Mr Mandavils and went to the hospital at Robinsons

---

[1] Rufus Chapman, tenth child of Stephen and Leuriah (Sanger) Chapman, was born Oct. 26, 1744, and died in May, 1848. He was married May 19, 1770, to Dorcas Sewall, of Exeter; they had one daughter. He is said to have charged his wife with being a witch, and he separated from her. He was a member of Capt. Stephen Kimball's Company, in Col. Daniel Hitchcock's Regiment, of the Army of Observation, 1775. See my " Revolutionary Defences in Rhode Island," page 6. Rufus Chapman was pensioned June 26, 1819, as a private of the Rhode Island Line. — *Senate Documents Pension Roll.*

Hous[1] returned to our Quarters in the Evening this Day was Clowdy but did not storm.

March 7th, 1781. A stormy morning with Snow & Rain after breakfast Col. Greene went for west Point but it stormed so that I thought it best to remain where I was which I did the Day.

8th March, 1781. Went over to the Point this morning after breakfast in the afternoon went for New Winsor in a Boat where I arrived about Eight o'clock in the Evening.

9th March. Clear Breakfasted with the Adj. General then paid off what men there was here then went to Newburgh in the Gen[l] [   ] Returned in the Evening.

10th. Left winsor this morning after Breakfast in a Boat with some Country people went to west point it Snowed the great part of the passage which made it very Dissagreable the Distance being about 8 miles I arrived at

---

[1] The Robinson House was the headquarters of Generals Putnam and Parsons in 1778-9. It took its name from Col. Beverly Robinson, its owner. What gives it more historic interest, however, is the fact that it was here, while at breakfast with his family and military guests, Benedict Arnold received the note from Colonel Jameson apprising him of the capture of Major André, and from whence he fled to the British sloop-of-war "Vulture." From this house General Washington wrote, Sept. 26, 1780, to General Heath informing him of the treason of Arnold. — *Heath's Memoirs, p. 253.*

Thatcher, in his Journal, under the date of April 12, 1781, writes that he "crossed the Hudson to the hospital at Robinson's House and passed the night with Dr. Eustis."

the Garrison about Two O'Clock Dined then went over to Mr Mandavells there tarried.

11th March, 1781. Clear plesant weather over head but bad under foot after breakfast I and Col Greene went to the point where we spent the Day in the afternoon Come over and went up upon the Mountain to the North Redoubt ¹ then to our Quarters.

March 12th, 1781. Good weather after Breakfast I sett of for the hutts where I din'd & spent the Day.

13th. Cold and windy this Day there was an Allarm on which the Militia was called to-geather but it proving to be a false Allarm they were Dismist.

14th. Clowdy and raind this Day nothing Remarkable

15th. A pleasant Morning but Soon Clowded over and raind in the afternoon the horses Sent for to Carry my Baggage to Rhode Island. News came this evening Arnold and his party was taken.

---

¹ The North Redoubt at West Point had an armament of three iron eighteen-pounders and three iron twelve-pounders. It is thus described in the " Remarks on Works at West Point " : " North Re-doubt, on the East side, built of stone 4 feet high ; above the stone, wood filled in with Earth, very Dry. No ditch : a Bomb Proof, three Batteries within the Fort, a poor Abattis a Rising piece of ground 500 yards So. the approaches Under Cover to within 20 yards. The work easily fired with Faggots dipt in Pitch &c."

16th. Good weather my Baggage Set off this morning for Rhode Island after Breakfast I set off for west Point went to Mr. Mandavills where I tarried.

17th March, 1781. Good weather a great parade this day with the Irish it being St Pataricks. I spent the day on the point and Tarried with the Officers.

18th. After Breakfast I set off on my Jorney for New England went to Mr Mandavills there Dind then went to Mrs Brewers my old Quarters this day was more like April than March

19th. Clowdy and Rained a little after Breakfast I set off went to the hutts there having some business which detained me till after Dinner. When I set off for Danbury where I arrived in the Evening it rained all the Afternoon very hard and worse riding could not be.

20th March, 1781. Clear good weather over head but muddy under foot after breakfast set forward went as far as Bostic there put up for the night having overtaken my waggon.

21st. Clear and Good weather after Breakfast went on as far as Southerington there dined at Curtisses Tavern then went to Mr. Coles in Farmington there put up for the night.

22d March, 1781. Left my lodgings after Breakfast went to hartford met with Capt Humphrey tarried there was obliged to hire a hors to help me on as far as hartford.

23d. A Stormy morning Crost the ferry to East Hartford, breakfasted went on to Hill's Tavern 8 mile there Halted for the waggon to come up which did not Arive till 3 o'clock the horses being tired out I hired a man to help me on as far as bolton where I halted that night.

24th. This morning being Clear there come two teams early a going to Canterbury and hired them to help me on upwards of twenty miles I rode on as far as Canterbury Stopt and Din'd in Scottand Put up at Landlord Back-uses but the waggon Didnot git up till the morning following.

25th March, 1781. Clear and Cold My waggon Come up this Morning after breakfast I set forward after having hired Capt Cacon to help me on as far as Dorrances in Vollen-town where I arrived and Dined then went on to my own hous found my family well. left my waggon to come on as fast as possible and thus Eands the Service with me. [1]

---

[1] By the Act of Congress of Oct. 3, 1780, the two Continental Regiments of Rhode Island were reduced to one, to take effect Jan. 1, 1781. By this arrangement Colonel Angell retired, and

26th March. Clear and Cold but soon Clowded over I hired Peleg Peck to go help my waggon on which arrived in the Evening.

27th March, 1781. After Breakfast I set off for Providence where I spent the Day at Evening went to my fathers and tarried news Come of the french fleet returning.

28th. Spent the forenoon at my fathers it being Exceeding Cold and unpleasant after Dinner went to Providence was informed that the french fleet was actually return'd and had had an Engagement with the English fleet but the particulars was not known one Circumstance in my journal of yesterday I forgot to mention that is I had the Pleasure of seeing Uncle James Angell, at my fathers who had not been there in 22 years before on acct. of some misunderstanding between him and my father.

29th March, 1781. Cold and Clowdy Snowed some but cleared off in the afternoon with a severe March wind and cold.

30th March. Clear and Cold with a violent high wind Nothing Remarkable.

31st. A tollerable pleasant day after

Christopher Green succeeded to the colonelcy of the consolidated regiment, who was succeeded a few months later by Lieut.-Col. Commandant Jeremiah Olney.

Breakfast I went to Providence where it was currently Reported that the french fleet behaved Gallantly in the action with ·the british and that the English fleet ran away from them Returned in the Evening.

April 1st, 1781. Clear and Spring like weather this morning but Soon Clowded over and the wind blew up at South very raw and Cold there was a meating held at my hous this day

2d. A violint Storm Set in last night and Continued this Day the Storm begun with Snow but before the middle of the Day turn'd to rain and by night had carried off the Greatest part of the Snow.

3d. It Still Continued Storming and had Snowed the Greatest part of the night and was a Considerable of Snow on the Ground but there being so much water made it Shocking Traveling.

INDEX.